Quipus and Witches' Knots

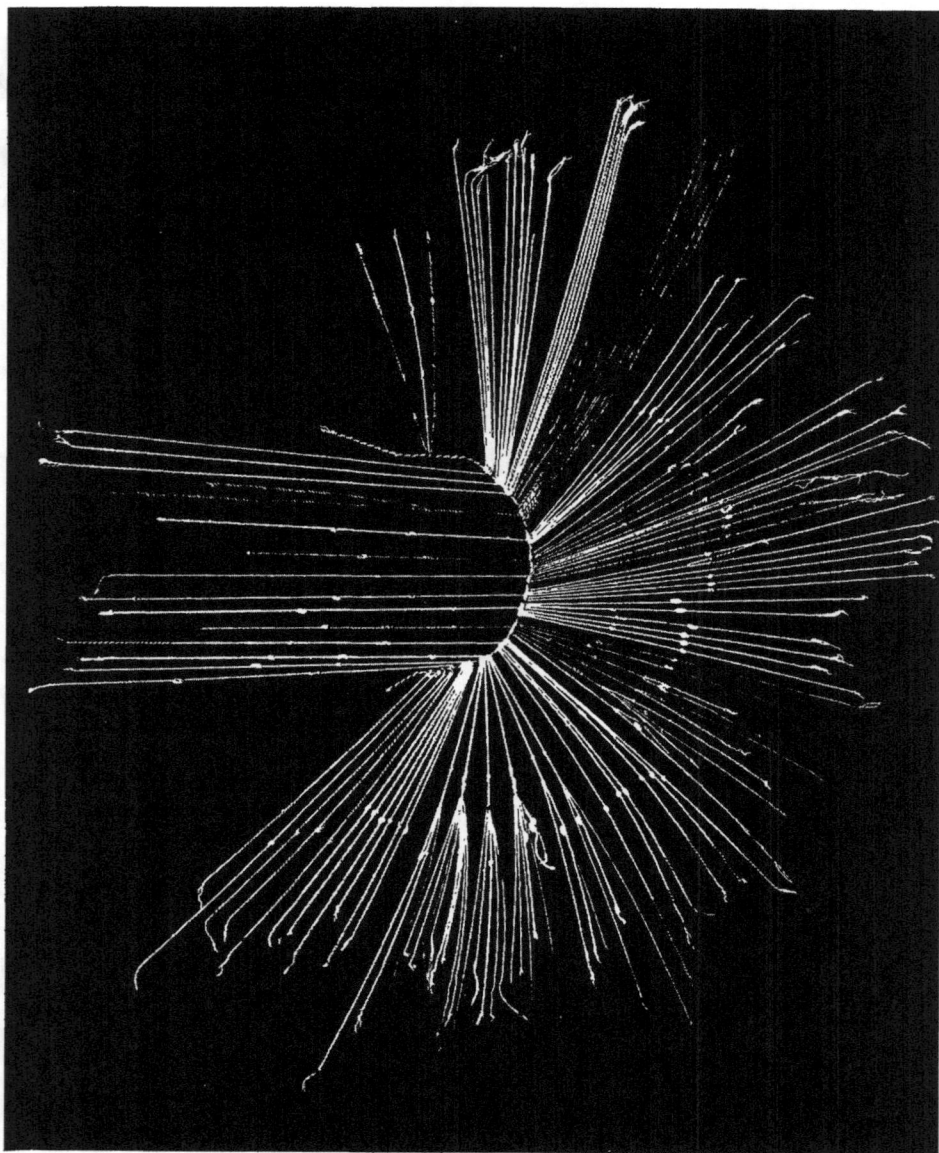

Quipus and Witches' Knots

THE ROLE OF THE KNOT IN PRIMITIVE AND ANCIENT CULTURES

With a Translation and Analysis of
"Oribasius *De Laqueis*"

By Cyrus Lawrence Day

The University of Kansas Press
Lawrence
1967

Published by the University Press of Kansas (Lawrence, Kansas 66045), which
was organized by the Kansas Board of Regents and is operated and funded by
Emporia State University, Fort Hays State University, Kansas State University,
Pittsburg State University, the University of Kansas, and Wichita State University.

Open access edition funded by the National Endowment for Humanities and the
Andrew W. Mellon Foundation Humanities Open Book Program.

Typographical errors may have been introduced in the digitization process.

Library of Congress Cataloging-in-Publication Data

Day, Cyrus Lawrence, 1900–1968
Quipus and witches' knots; the role of the knot in primitive
and ancient cultures. With a translation and analysis of "Oribasius. De laqueis."
ISBN 978-0-7006-0019-9 (cloth)
ISBN 978-0-7006-3146-9 (paperback)
ISBN 978-0-7006-3083-7 (ebook)
GR950.K6 D3   398.3/5
LC record available at https://lccn.loc.gov/67018736.

British Library Cataloguing in Publication Data is available.

Printed in the United States of America

The paper used in this publication meets the minimum requirements of
the American National Standard for Permanence of Paper for
Printed Library Materials Z39.48-1984.

And
This Too Is For
Camilla

Acknowledgments

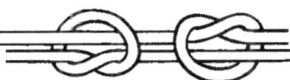

I am indebted to the editors of *Western Folklore* for permitting me to make use of portions of two essays which I wrote for their journal in 1950 and 1957: "Knots and Knot Lore—A Study in Primitive Beliefs and Superstitions," *Western Folklore*, IX (July, 1950), 229-256, and "Knots and Knot Lore—Quipus and Other Mnemonic Knots," *Western Folklore*, XVI (January, 1957), 8-26.

I wish also to thank the following friends and acquaintances for their generosity in putting their specialized knowledge at my disposal and answering my all-too numerous queries: Miss Ruth Alford, Dr. Palle Birkelund, Dr. Junius Bird, Mr. W. H. Bohning, Miss Virginia Burton, Dr. Schuyler Cammann, Dr. Frederick J. Dockstader, Dr. Henry G. Fischer, Mrs. Caroline Groot, Miss Eleanore Hofstetter, Dr. Robert Jackson, Mr. W. B. McDaniel II, Dr. Kimberley Roberts, Dr. Carl G. Stridbeck, Dr. A. T. Valbuena Briones, Dr. Gordon L. Walker, Dr. Henry Wassén, and Mr. John Wise. And more particularly I wish to thank Miss Milica Dimitrijevic for helping me to read the quipus in the American Museum of Natural History and the Museum of the American Indian; Professor Frank Zozzora for advising me on the preparation of the illustrative drawings; and Dr. Evelyn H. Clift and Dr. William J. Fletcher for resolving several linguistic difficulties which I encountered in my translation of Heraklas's Greek text.

C.D.

June 21, 1966

Contents

Chapter Three: Practical Knots

Chapter One: Mnemonic Knots

1. KNOT-CALENDARS

THE HUMAN MEMORY may be compared to a complex and capacious but untidy filing cabinet. It stores up all kinds of impressions, pleasant and unpleasant, but it does not catalogue them very systematically. It stores up facts, figures, information, and misinformation. It makes cultural continuity and progress possible, but only to the extent that each individual is able to transmit what he knows to his personal associates and successors. If the human memory had not been supplemented by the mechanical memory of books and libraries, we would still be living today in a state of idyllic (or was it merely barbaric?) tribal simplicity.

Before writing was invented, primitive man used knots to supplement his fallible human memory. Knots are a clumsy mnemonic device compared to writing, but it is easy to see why primitive man should have had recourse to them. They were at hand, available, constantly present before his eyes—a tool he relied on and was familiar with. He tied knots every day of his life, not only to secure and join material things—fishlines and fishhooks, for example—but also, in his magic rites, to bind and control intangible, immaterial things, like the demons of disease and the spirits of the dead. Binding the figments of his memory, storing them in the firm grasp of knots, would have seemed, to primitive man, a reasonable and practical thing to do.

Mnemonic knots as utilized by primitive man had two chief functions: (1) numerical—to record dates and numbers; and (2) cultural—to help preserve the memory of songs, stories, genealogies, historical traditions, and religious laws.

Numerical knots, in their simplest and probably earliest form, consisted of knotted strings or thongs by means of which a person or group of persons could keep track of dates and the passage of time—in a word,

1

knot-calendars. Cultural knots are more difficult than numerical knots for modern literate man to understand. They once played a vital role, nevertheless, in the lives of primitive people in many parts of the world.

Herodotus provides us with what is probably the oldest account of the way knot-calendars were once used. The Persian king Darius, after crossing the River Ister in order to attack the Scythians, accepted the advice of Coës to leave a guard at the bridge. Whereupon he tied "sixty knots in a thong, and calling the despots of the Ionians to an audience he said to them: 'Ionians, I renounce the opinion which I before declared concerning the bridge; do you now take this thong and do as I command you. Begin to reckon from the day when you shall see me march away against the Scythians, and loose one knot each day: and if the days marked by the knots have all passed and I have not returned ere then, take ship for your own homes.' "[1]

Knot-calendars were on ancient device, presumably, even in Herodotus's day. More than two thousand years later they were still being used in Asia, Africa, the two Americas, and the Islands of the Pacific. The knotted handkerchief and the string tied round the finger are evidence that they were once used, also, in Europe. A few examples from among the many that could be cited will serve to illustrate their principal functions and their worldwide distribution.

Early in the present century a native of the Makonde Plateau in East Africa showed Karl Weule a piece of bark string with eleven knots in it. If he were going on a journey of eleven days, he said, he would leave the string with his wife and tell her that the first knot represented the day of his departure and the next three knots the days when he would be traveling. Here, he would tell her (pointing to the fifth knot), he would reach his destination, and here (touching the sixth knot) he would transact his business. On the seventh day he would start for home.

"Do not forget, wife," he would say, "to undo a knot every day, and on the tenth you will have to cook food for me; for, see, this is the eleventh day when I shall come back."[2]

In India during the eighteenth century, the inhabitants of the hills near Rajamahall in Bengal marked the dates of festivals by means of knotted strings which were sent to all the invited guests. One knot in each string was cut off each day, and when only one knot remained, the guests knew that the day for the festival was at hand.[3] And in much the same way, when a marriage was being arranged among the primitive Khonds, a Dravidian tribe of southern India, knotted strings were given (perhaps still are given) to the family of the bride and to the representatives of the groom ("the searchers for the bride"), and the date of the betrothal ceremony was kept in mind by the untying, in both strings, of a knot each day.[4]

The Pueblo Indians of New Mexico and Arizona, in 1680, tried to synchronize a general uprising against the Spaniards by means of knotted strings. The rebel leader, a medicine man named Popé, of the San Juan Pueblo, chose August 13 as the date for the proposed attack. Runners then carried knotted strings to all the other pueblos, "even to the far-off Hopi in Arizona." News of the plan leaked out, however, and the attack was prematurely launched on August 10. Twenty-one of thirty-three missionaries were killed, and about 375 colonists.[5]

Ten years earlier, in 1670, John Lederer, a German intellectual and the first European to explore the Virginia and North Carolina Piedmont, observed that the Indians kept "an account of Time, and other things"—one could wish he had been more specific—"on a string or leather thong in knots of several colours."[6]

The "other things" probably included furs and pelts, for the surveyor John Lawson remarks in his *History of North Carolina* (1714) that "James had sent Knots to all the Indians thereabouts, for every Town to send in ten Skins"—meaning, he adds, "Captain Moor, then Governor of South Carolina."[7] James Moore, who died in 1706, had tried while governor to monopolize the Indian fur trade.

James Adair, an eighteenth-century trader who lived for many years with the Choctaws and other Eastern tribes, said in 1775 that the Indians used knots "of various colors and makes" in order to number the winters, the moons, and the days, and in order to fix the dates of "certain secret intended acts of hostility":

"Under such circumstances, if one day elapses, each of them loosens a knot, or cuts off a notch, or else makes one, according to previous agreement; which those who are in the trading way among them call broken days. Thus they proceed day by day, till the whole time is expired, which was marked out, or agreed upon; and they know with

3

certainty, the exact time of any of the aforesaid periods, when they are to execute their secret purposes."[8]

A remarkable instance of the use of synchronized knot-calendars is described by Lumholtz in his book on the primitive peoples of modern Mexico. The Huichol Indians, a conservative tribe, undertake a semi-annual pilgrimage in search of the *hikuli,* or sacred cactus. The leader of the pilgrimage carries a string with a number of knots in it, and one of the principal men remains behind in the temple and follows the pilgrims in his thoughts with the aid of an equal number of knots in a similar string. One knot in each string is untied each day, and in this way the pilgrims keep in spiritual touch with the people at home, and are protected, so they believe, from harm:

"When the hikuli-seekers return, each of them puts the string calendar twice across his back, once around each foot, once around the body, then down to each knee. This is done inside of the temple, and the watchman [i. e., the man who has remained behind] does the same with his calendar; thereupon both calendars are burnt."[9]

The Pueblo Indians were still using knot-calendars as recently as the 1920's. Spier reports that a string with seventeen knots in it, made by the "policeman" of the Havasupai reservation, was sent to a Navaho village in September, 1919, together with an invitation to attend a Havasupai dance; and on August 26, 1921, a Navaho sent ten knots in a string to the Havasupai by way of announcing that they could expect a visit from his people on September 4.[10]

"Old Sally Jackson," a Yakima Indian of the State of Washington, made a calendrical knot-record of the deaths in her family between 1915 and 1919. Groups of seven knots, set apart by red woolen markers, represented weeks. The record, when she sold it, was 35 feet long and contained 1,577 knots. She tied the last knot on June 30, 1919.[11]

Knot-calendars were once familiar objects in the South Pacific. Mid-afternoon in the Solomon Islands was called "the time of the tying of the knot." The lunar month began with the rising of the new moon, and when a chieftain died, thirty knots were tied in a string, or thirty notches were cut in a stick of wood, to mark the number of new moons until the *didiaugo* or funeral feast in honor of the chieftain's memory. When an unimportant person died, only three or four knots were tied, representing a mourning period of only three or four moons.[12]

The crew of an American whaling ship, in 1829, kidnaped the son of a Marquesan chieftain. A knot was tied in a string at every full moon thereafter, and when Charles Stewart saw the string a few months later, it already had five knots in it, "pointing out the month of March, as the period of this infamous visit."[13]

2. LEE BOO AND HIS "LINE"

Knot-calendars are as good a way as any, it would seem, to remind a primitive man of his military and social engagements—provided he can remember to untie a knot a day. But in societies of any complexity, men feel the need to preserve many other kinds of information; and before writing was invented, mnemonic knots were pressed into service as records and reminders of a wide variety of facts, figures, and verbal lore.

An instructive illustration of what primitive people thought mnemonic knots could accomplish is found in George Keate's eighteenth-century account of the Palau Islands.[14] Captain Wilson and his crew, following the loss of their ship, were entertained by Abba Thulle, a native king; and when they were ready to depart in a new ship they had built, Abba Thulle's second son, a boy named Lee Boo, obtained his father's permission to accompany them to England, on condition that Captain Wilson would treat him as his own son. The evening before the ship sailed, Abba Thulle asked Captain Wilson how long it might be before his return to the Islands. "And being told, that it would probably be about thirty moons, or might chance to extend to six more, *Abba Thulle* drew from his basket a piece of *Line*, and, after making thirty knots on it, a little distance from each other, left a long space, and then, adding six others, carefully put it by."

Abba Thulle was using a conventional knot-calendar. On board ship, his son attempted something more ambitious. He was extremely desirous, says Keate, "of knowing the name and country of every ship he met at sea, and would repeat what he was told over and over till he had fixed it well in his memory; and, as each inquiry was gratified, he made a knot on his *Line*; but these knots now having greatly multiplied, he was obliged to repeat them over every day to refresh his memory, and often to recur to Captain *Wilson*, or others, when he had forgot what any particular knot referred to. The officers in the *Morse* . . .

when they saw him busied with his *Line,* used to say that he was reading his journal."

Lee Boo soon perceived that writing was a better mechanical memory than a knotted string. He persuaded Captain Wilson to teach him the alphabet, and to send him to school in England, where he died of smallpox, a victim of the civilization he so ardently admired. His father, waiting in Palau for the boy's return, was destined to untie his thirty-six knots in vain.

It is difficult for a literate person to see how Lee Boo's knots could have helped him to remember a long list of names. If he had merely wanted to record the *number* of the ships he met, his knots would have served him very well. But information other than numerical cannot reside in knots, or at any rate is not explicit in knots, in the sense that it is explicit in writing. Moreover all Lee Boo's knots were presumably alike (i. e., overhand knots if his "line" resembled other Polynesian string-records). Hence the association in his mind between a particular knot and a particular ship must have been as uncertain as it was arbitrary. It is understandable that he should have had trouble committing his catalogue of ships to memory.

Association, nevertheless, is the principle by which knot-records seem to have operated—in somewhat the same way, perhaps, that the number of a Mosaic Commandment (the analogy is Prescott's[15]) calls to mind the Commandment itself—or, to cite a modern instance, that the characteristics of the cross streets in New York are linked in the consciousness of New Yorkers with the numbers by which the streets are designated. Other principles of memory that must have been employed were interest, concentration, and repetition. Keate implies that Lee Boo depended (instinctively, of course) on all of them.

It is also possible that slight differences in the knots of a given string-record—differences resulting from irregularities in the thickness, texture, twist, and coloration of homemade strings—may have helped to recall the names associated with particular knots, even though all the knots were of the same type. I have seen a four-year-old boy who could identify phonograph records by holding them up to the light and studying the patterns of the grooves, and in like manner the owner of a cherished and often-examined string-record could, perhaps, distinguish one knot from another by means of peculiarities that a casual observer would fail to notice. An extension of this principle would lead to the use of cords and knots of different kinds and colors, a development that took place in Hawaii, Peru, and elsewhere.

3. POLYNESIAN KNOT-RECORDS

Knot-records analogous to Lee Boo's "line" were used in the Marquesas Islands until the second half of the nineteenth century to "record" genealogies, folk-songs, and legends. Paul Clavérie, who visited the Marquesas in 1881 and 1882, was shown a record that purported to trace the descent of a certain high priest back to the first man and the first woman. Every knot was identified with the name of an ancestor; and the priest, with the string in his hand, proceeded from knot to knot, giving each the name of one of his ancestors, until at length he came to himself.[16]

Some years later Karl von den Steinen saw a Marquesan knot-genealogy that went back 159 generations, or (counting thirty years to a generation) to about 2870 B. C. The Mikado of Japan, he remarks, is a mere parvenu compared with some of the unlettered princelings of the Pacific islands; for the family trees of the Marquesans go back to the earliest colonization of the archipelago, to the gods in Hawaiki (the legendary homeland of the race), and even to the myths of the creation of the universe.[17]

A typical Marquesan knot-record consisted of a hollow plaited core called the *toó* (Steinen translates *toó* by the German *Knäuel*), to which various appendages, including knotted strings, were attached. The *toó* represented the earth and "contained" the history of the gods. Steinen includes photographs, in his book, of eight specimens. The most elaborate has nineteen strings, of which seven were for songs, according to the woman who had owned it, and twelve were for genealogies. Another specimen has two strings, with about 150 knots in one of them, and about 290 knots in the other.

Specimen no. 5 in Steinen's book has a *toó* about the size of a baby's head, and a single string containing about 245 knots. It was used, Steinen says, as follows: "Many genealogical lists and many stories"—he was told—"are contained in the empty *toó*. The *tuhuka* or priest asked the people who were sitting round him: 'What story do you want?' Then he looked thoughtfully at the *toó* for a moment and began the required story, which he knew by heart." This passage sheds regrettably little light on the psychological service rendered either by the *toó* or by the knots attached to it. Since the *tuhuka* knew the story by heart, and since his audience selected the story they wanted to hear, one wonders why a knot-record was necessary at all.

In earlier times, Steinen was told, a post with knots tied to it stood on the western cape of the island of Hivoa. There the souls of the dead leaped from the cliff into the sea, in order to begin their post-mortal journey to the homeland (Hawaiki); and a priest was appointed to register, by means of an additional knot, every death that came to his notice. This custom provides a modicum of support for the traditional view that the Polynesians originated in Asia and not in South America. Primitive people are not apt to confuse the east and the west.

A folk tale from Samoa recounts the victory of the little fishes in individual combat with the big fishes. The mano'o, a little fish, chose to fight the porpoise. The porpoise advanced, uttering abusive insults, but the mano'o leaped into his nostril and began to wriggle. The porpoise admitted defeat. Thereupon "King Tapakea praised mano'o for bravery, and called out to the onlookers on the beach to mark mano'o as victorious. This *marking* was done by setting up a cocoa-nut leaf, and tying a knot on the top of it. Tying a number of knots on a piece of cord was also a common way of noting and remembering things, in the absence of a written language, among these South Sea Islanders."[18]

In Hawaii an extraordinary "tax-gatherer's memorandum cord" was seen by Tyerman and Bennet in 1822.

> The tax-gatherers, though they can neither read nor write, keep very exact accounts of all the articles, of all kinds, collected from the inhabitants throughout the island. This is done principally by one man, and the register is nothing more than a line of cordage from four to five hundred fathoms in length. Distinct portions of this are allotted to the various districts, which are known one from another by knots, loops, and tufts, of different shapes, sizes, and colors. Each tax-payer in the district has his part in this string, and the number of dollars, hogs, dogs, pieces of sandal-wood, quantity of taro, &c, at which he is rated, is well defined by means of marks, of the above

kinds, most ingeniously diversified. It is probable that the famous *quippos,* or system of knots, whereby the records of the ancient Peruvian empire are said to have been kept, were a similar, and perhaps not much more comprehensive, mode of reckoning dates and associating names with historical events.[19]

The most distinctive characteristic of this cord, aside from its astonishing length—nearly half a mile—is the fact that the knots, loops, and other objects attached to it were of different kinds, colors, and materials. Hence anyone who knew the code could "read" it, for the knots and other objects not only served as reminders, but also provided information. The Marquesan cords, described above, could be interpreted only by their makers, or by persons whom their makers had instructed.

4. MISCELLANEOUS KNOT-RECORDS

During the time when the Huichol Indians in Mexico were away on a pilgrimage in search of the sacred *hikuli,* or drinking gourd of the God of Fire (see above, p. 4), the women at home made public confession of all their sins. If a woman left out a single sin, no matter how long ago she had committed it, the pilgrims would have been unable to find a single *hikuli.* To bolster her memory, each woman tied as many knots in a palm-leaf string as she had had lovers. Then, standing in the temple before the sacred fire, she named, one by one, all the men recorded on her string, threw the string into the fire, and considered herself purified and forgiven.[20]

The pilgrims recorded their sins in the same manner, and upon reaching a place called La Puerta de Cerda, they first talked "to all the five winds," and then delivered their "roll calls" to their leader, who cast them into the fire. One of the pilgrims told Lumholtz, who describes the custom, that his string contained twelve knots, besides seven for women who had merely caught him by the hand or arm.

In India the Santals in the more remote parts of Santal Parganas used to take the census with knots on cords of four different colors—black for adult men, red for adult women, white for boys, and yellow for girls. The headman who took the census, being unable to read or write, "simply followed the popular method of keeping a numerical account."[21]

The Arapaho Indians, an Algonquin tribe, commemorated their participation in the ceremony of the dog dance by means of knots. The procedure was formal and complicated.

> Every morning each dancer, accompanied by his wife, repairs to his grandfather. His grandfather has a string with a number of knots on it, representing the number of times he was painted when he went through the ceremony. This number is often about forty, but sometimes it runs as high as ninety. Every time the grandfather paints the dancer he unties one knot in his string. At the same time the younger man makes a knot in a string which he brings. At the end of the painting the grandfather has untied all the knots in his string; and the grandson's string now contains the same number, which, when he in turn becomes the grandfather of a later dancer will be untied in the same way.[22]

Knot-records were formerly used on the Ryukyu Islands, according to Simon,[23] for tax receipts, census reports, laborers' accounts, and inventories of harvests. But writing as taught in Japanese schools was rapidly superseding them before the beginning of World War I. Pawnbrokers on Okinawa, however, continued to record the dates and amounts of loans by means of knots on strings of grass and bast. The months (the first to the ninth) were indicated by from one to nine overhand knots in the upper half of the string. The tenth month was indicated by a loop knot, the eleventh by a loop knot plus an overhand knot, and the twelfth by a loop knot plus two overhand knots.

The amount of the loan was recorded on the lower half of the string. If decimals were required, knots were tied in subsidiary strings, formed either by splitting the main string, or by tying another string to the main string at the appropriate place.

Simon pictures an ingenious "letter of instruction" in the form of knots sent by an Okinawa employer to a woodcutter in the mountains. A leaf inserted in the device indicated the species of tree to be cut. Knots at predetermined places indicated the quantity, length, width, and thickness of the required pieces of timber.

Knot-records were superseded by writing at a very early date in the most civilized parts of the world. The transition was almost complete in China by the sixth century B. C., and we have only a few bits of evidence that they had formerly been used there. Lao-tse refers to them in enigmatical terms of praise which Wai-Tao and Goddard translate as follows: "Let people return to the spirit of the olden days when they used knotted cords for their records."[24]

Further evidence is supplied by two ancient tablets that depict knots representing numbers, "odd numbers being designated by white knots (standing for complete, as day, warmth, the sun) while even numbers are designated by black knots (standing for incomplete, as night, cold, water, earth)."[25] There is an unsubstantiated tradition, also, that knotted cords were used in China for keeping accounts as late as 200 B. C.[26]

On the Gold Coast of Africa in the 1720's (to cite a characteristic modern example), the upper-class Negroes were learning to read and write the Portuguese language, but the uneducated masses continued to rely on knotted cords. "The people do not know how to read or write," a French observer remarked in 1730. "Instead, they have little knotted cords, the knots of which have meaning. Knots of this sort are used by several tribes of American savages. People of importance all know the Portuguese language, and read and write it well."[27]

5. PHYLACTERIES AND FRINGES

The ancient Hebrews used mnemonic knots before they adopted an alphabet and a system of writing, and in the opinion of the late Professor Gandz, the phylacteries and knotted fringes of Jewish ritual are the lineal descendants of primitive knot-records which served in prehistoric times as *memoria technica* for the purpose of perpetuating history, tradition, and codes of law.[28]

Phylacteries are small leather boxes which contain passages from Hebrew Scripture. They are fixed on the forehead and the left arm by means of knots shaped like the letters *daleth* and *yod,* and the evidence of the Bible, according to Gandz, indicates that the knots originally played the central role in them. Thus Deuteronomy 6:6-9 reads as follows:

"And these words, which I command thee this day, shall be in thine heart: And thou shalt teach them diligently unto thy children, and shalt talk of them when thou sittest in thine house, and when thou walkest by the way, and when thou liest down, and when thou risest up. And thou shalt bind them for a sign upon thine hand, and they shall be as frontlets between thine eyes. And thou shalt write them upon the posts of thy house, and on thy gates."

The lawgiver, says Gandz, wants his laws to be remembered. "So he enjoins his people to preserve them well in their hearts, and to hand them over to their children by oral tradition. He orders them to repeat and memorize these commandments, to strengthen their memory by knots and mnemonic signs . . . and to write them down." Thus the three ways of preserving old traditions are represented: (1) the repetition and transmission of verbal lore to the children; (2) mnemonic knots and signs; and (3) writing.

The blue-and-white knotted fringes of Jewish ritual are even more convincing evidence, in Gandz's opinion, of the use of mnemonic knots in prehistoric times. Numbers 15:38-39, for example, reads as follows: "Speak unto the children of Israel, and bid them that they make them fringes in the borders of their garments throughout their generations, and that they put upon the fringe of the borders a ribband of blue: And it shall be unto you for a fringe, that you may look upon it, and remember all the commandments of the Lord, and do them. . . ."

"There can be no doubt," says Gandz, "that the fringe, with the threads of blue and white wool twisted to a cord and having five double knots at different distances, of which the outspoken purpose is that the people may look upon them and remember the commandments, represents the vestigial remnant of the old Hebrew quipu, that served to record the laws, traditions, and historical events."

6. Abacus, Rosary, and Log Line

Gandz has suggested that the knotted cord preceded the dust board and the abacus for purposes of mathematical computations. It has generally been assumed, he says, that the word "abacus" means "dust board," and that it is derived from the Hebrew word *abaq* (dust).

"Now the Hebrew-Aramaic word *abaq* has two roots. The one meaning 'dust, powder,' or 'to cover with dust,' and the other signifying 'a loop, knot,' or 'to make a loop or knot, to twist, twine, to be attached, to cling to.'

"The probability, therefore, . . . is that the term abacus does not belong to the first root, meaning dust, but to the second root, meaning knot, and that it was applied, originally, to the knotted cord."[29]

Other ancient languages, Gandz believes, support his suggestion. In Arabic the tens and hundreds are called knots ('uqûd). Al-Khwarizmi, ninth-century mathematician, said that numbers consist of units, knots, and composites. The Romans said they consist of digits, articles or joints (articuli), and composites; and Gandz holds that the word articuli should be translated by the word "knots," for, he says, its original meaning was "knots that join and bind the bones of the fingers." Knotted cords, if Gandz's conjectures are valid, were the first mechanical computers.

Knotted cords, however, are not, by their very nature, a convenient device by means of which to perform a mathematical computation. Knots take time to tie, and even more time to untie; and knotted cords (the cords of Peruvian quipus, for example), tend to get intolerably tangled up with each other when handled and manipulated. The counters on a dust board and the buttons on an abacus, on the other hand, can be speedily and accurately removed, replaced, and rearranged as the successive steps in a mathematical computation are performed. Gandz's linguistic evidence is impressive, but knotted strings, however convenient as a way of *recording* the *results* of computations, could never have been widely used (in my opinion) as *computers*.

Strings *without* knots, it must be admitted, were used as computers not very long ago on the Ryukyu Islands.[30] The native grooms who loaded merchandise on packhorses had tassel-like devices attached to their belts, and to compute prices and costs they manipulated the strings of the tassels between their fingers in a way that distinguished the units, tens, hundreds, and thousands from one another. Thus to express the number 1253 they would grasp a single string between the thumb and the forefinger, two strings between the forefinger and the middle finger, five strings between the middle finger and the ring finger, and three strings between the ring finger and the little finger. To add to this number, they would add strings, as needed, to the groups between the appropriate fingers, "carrying" digits when a number reached ten, much as the buttons are manipulated on an abacus.

These tassels, being knotless, lend little support, if any, to Gandz's thesis. The oriental rosary and the mariner's log line, however, both

13

of which make use of knots, may be regarded as elementary kinds of computers. The rosary probably originated in Asia, and was made with knots, at first, rather than with beads. The Sikhs of India still use a rosary of 108 knots tied in a woolen cord, and the Greek Orthodox monks of Mount Athos use a rosary of 100 knots divided into equal parts by four large beads. As defined by Winifred Blackman, a rosary is "a string of knots or beads, designed as an aid to the memory, and providing a convenient method for counting the recitations of prayers or the repetition of the names and attributes of the Deity."[31]

The mariner's log line, a device for measuring a vessel's speed through the water, is a comparatively modern invention. It consists of a light line or rope that is divided into 47-foot 3-inch lengths, called knots, by means of pieces of cord inserted between the strands and knotted with the number of knots corresponding to the number of 47-foot 3-inch lengths from the end of the line. A piece of wood called the chip, which is attached to the end of the line, is cast overboard and acts as a drag that remains more or less stationary in the water. The line runs out astern, therefore, as the vessel moves ahead, and the number of knots that pass through the mariner's hands while a 28-second glass empties itself is the speed of the vessel in nautical miles an hour. The clipper ship *Flying Cloud* once "ran out" eighteen knots on the log line, and there was still a little sand left in the glass.

7. THE PERUVIAN QUIPU (LOCKE'S ANALYSIS)

The Inca empire of pre-Spanish Peru, diverse in climate, difficult in terrain, and vast in extent—three thousand miles long from north to south, in fact, at the time of the death in 1525 of the Inca Huayna Capac —had been conquered and was administered without benefit of the wheel, the draft animal, or the written word. Its material culture, which dazzled the eyes of the Spanish Conquistadors, was an inheritance, in large measure, from the indigenous past, exploited by the Incas with spectacular success, but not originated by them. Textiles of remarkable artistic and technical excellence, for example, had been produced in Peru ever since as early as 3000 B. C. And the celebrated Peruvian quipus which the Inca bureaucracy relied on (in default of a system of writing) to keep their detailed accounts and records, were probably

14

not an entirely new invention (in my opinion), but rather an ingenious and sophisticated elaboration of the mnemonic knot-records and knot-calendars which, as we have seen, were once used by primitive people in all parts of the world.

"Quipu" is a Quechua word meaning "knot." A typical quipu, as described by the sixteenth-century Spanish chroniclers, and as represented by extant specimens in archaeological museums, consisted of a number of vertical or pendent cords, more or less like a fringe, suspended from a horizontal or main cord. Subsidiary cords, more or less like the branches of a stream, were sometimes attached to pendent cords. Knots representing numbers were tied in pendent and subsidiary cords, and occasionally in main cords.

The Peruvian Indians used a decimal system of numeration, and (in their quipus) a system of notation by position. "They counted from one to ten" on their knots, wrote Cieza de León in 1553, "and from ten to a hundred, and from a hundred to a thousand."[32]

And Garcilaso "el Inca," the offspring of an aristocratic Spaniard and an Inca princess (a niece, in fact, of the Inca Huayna Capac), who learned about the traditions of his race from the members of his mother's family, describes the positional notation of the quipus with unmistakable clarity as follows:

"According to their position, the knots signified unities, tens, hundreds, thousands, ten thousands and, exceptionally, hundred thousands, and they were all as well aligned on their different cords as the figures that an accountant sets down, column by column, in his ledger."[33]

L. L. Locke, the foremost modern authority on the quipu, confirmed the accuracy of this statement of Garcilaso's in 1912 by means of a remarkable quipu in the American Museum of Natural History.[34] This quipu (No. B-8713 in the Museum's catalogue) has 24 pendent cords arranged in 6 groups of 4 cords each, and the cords in each group are held together by an additional cord which is looped into them at the top and which Locke calls a summation or top cord.

By spreading the quipu out and aligning the knots in horizontal rows, as suggested by Garcilaso, Locke was able to show that the knots near the lower ends of the cords represent the units, the knots in the middle the tens, and the knots at the top the hundreds. The summation cords, he found, validate this way of reading the quipu, for they

QUIPU KNOTS

LEFT-LAY OR S-TWIST	RIGHT-LAY OR Z-TWIST	TWO COLORS MIXED	TWO COLORS SPIRAL

OVERHAND KNOT

METHOD OF
ATTACHING
PENDENT
CORDS

FIGURE-EIGHT KNOT

PSEUDO FIGURE-EIGHT KNOT

FOUR-FOLD LONG KNOT LOOSE

PULLED TO LEFT AND PULLED BOTH WAYS

16

register, in each case, the sums of the numbers on the four cords in their respective groups.

Thus, cord 1 in group "a" of Quipu B-8713 is blank (value: 0). Cord 2 has a single overhand knot midway between the lower end and the upper end (value: 10). Cord 3 has a 6-fold long knot near the lower end (value: 6). Cord 4 has a single Flemish or figure-eight knot near the lower end (value: 1). The summation cord of group "a" has a single overhand knot midway between the ends (value: 10) and a 7-fold long knot near the lower end (value: 7). The sum of the numbers on the pendent cords is 17, and the number on the summation cord is likewise 17.

Locke showed, also, that the knots used to denote the units differ in kind from the knots used to denote the tens, hundreds, thousands, etc. Figure-eight knots (he calls them Flemish knots) customarily denote the number 1, and multiple overhand knots (he calls them long knots) customarily denote the numbers 2 to 9. Knots of these two kinds are found near the lower ends of pendent, subsidiary, and summation cords.

Overhand knots (Locke calls them single knots) denote the tens, hundreds, thousands, etc. Knots of this kind, tied close together in groups, are found higher on the cords. The absence of a knot in a horizontal row denotes the absence of number (i.e., zero). Only two people, the Indians of India and the Indians of America (Mayan and Peruvian), are credited with having invented ways to represent the mathematical concept of nothingness.

The summation cord of Group "c" in Quipu B-8713 illustrates the Peruvian Indian way of representing zero. A 5-fold long knot is tied near the lower end of the cord (value: 5), and 8 overhand or single knots are tied close together near the upper end of the cord (value: 800). There is no knot in the middle of the cord (value: 00). The number registered on the cord, therefore, is 805.

Diagrams of the chief kinds of knots used in extant quipus are provided on the facing page for the benefit of readers who are unfamiliar with knots and knot-nomenclature. The two forms of the long knot distinguished by Locke are shown at the bottom of the page. When tying the first form, a right-handed Indian probably would have held the loose turns in place with the fingers of his right hand, and pulled the cord to the left with his left hand, in the direction of the main cord, in order to tighten the knot. A left-handed Indian would have worked the other way. When tying the second form, an Indian would have pulled both ends (in opposite directions, of course) in order to tighten the knot. The first form is characteristic of the type of quipu found near Ica and Chancay; the second, of the type found in the vicinity of Cajamarquilla.

The diagrams on page 16 include a previously unidentified knot which is tied near the ends of seven cords in Quipu B-7808 in the American Museum of Natural History. Locke mistook this knot in five instances for a 2-fold long knot, and in two instances for a figure-eight knot. I have called it a pseudo figure-eight knot, since it looks something like a figure-eight knot, and evidently serves the same purpose—that is, it represents the number 1.

Most of the cords in extant quipus are made of two-ply S-twist (i.e., left lay) undyed cotton. A few are made of wool and even (very rarely) of a hard unidentifiable fiber. A few have Z-twist (i.e., right lay). The terms S- and Z-twist are convenient ways of denoting the twist or lay of a cord because the central strokes of the letters S and Z point to the left and right respectively. They point in the same directions, in other words, as the spiral grooves between the strands of left- and right-lay cords.

The predominant colors of the cords in extant quipus are dull white and various shades of brown. Locke, Nordenskiöld, Altieri,[35] and Primeglio[36] use the terms "white," "light brown," "brown," and "dark brown" to distinguish the colors from one another. It is not clear at the present time, however, whether small differences in the shade of the brown cords are significant or not. The symbolic color schemes mentioned by the early chroniclers (white for silver, yellow for gold, red for soldiers, and so on) do not seem to have been used in any extant quipus.

Locke's book *The Ancient Quipu*,[37] published in 1923, is the primary modern study of the quipu. It contains his demonstration (first published in 1912) that the knots on the cords of extant quipus (most of them, at any rate) represent numbers arranged according to a decimal system of notation; photographs of all the quipus owned in 1923 by the American Museum of Natural History; readings and schematic diagrams of two quipus numbered B-8713 and B-8715 in the Museum's catalogue; relevant excerpts from the writings of the Spanish chroniclers; and a judicious survey of the entire quipu problem.

Quipus, Locke concludes, were used for two chief purposes: (1) to record numbers and (2) to aid in the memorization of historical and cultural lore and traditions. They were *not* used, in his opinion, for mathematical computations, but rather to record the *results* of such computations. All the quipus studied by Locke, Nordenskiöld, and others seem to record numbers and therefore to belong to the first of the two foregoing categories.

8. The Peruvian Quipu (Nordenskiöld's Hypothesis)

In 1925, Erland Nordenskiöld,[38] the eminent Finnish ethnologist, published sixteen quipus which show (if his analysis is valid) that the Peruvian Indians had an accurate knowledge of the movements of the Sun and the Moon and of the planets Mercury, Venus, and Jupiter. The early chroniclers—Garcilaso[39] and Huaman Poma[40] in particular—speak of observations by the Indian astrologers of the Sun and the Moon in order to fix the dates of the agricultural and ritual years. Accurate observations of the movements of the planets imply a previously unsuspected degree of astronomical sophistication.

The sixteen quipus analyzed by Nordenskiöld were found in graves (like almost all extant quipus), and therefore, in his opinion, must have recorded something thought to be important to the dead—something, that is to say, of magical or religious significance.

Undoubtedly, says Nordenskiöld, the Indians used quipus for practical, everyday purposes (census reports and tax records, for example). But they would never have put a quipu containing information about the living into a grave. To have done so would have been tantamount to giving the dead power over the living. It would have been more consistent with Indian psychology, he argues, if the quipus found in graves contained numbers that the Indians considered magical.

"I think I can show," he says, "that the *numbers indicated days*," and that "these grave-quipus are calendars, and I regard it as highly probable that, like the Maya codices, they are nothing but books of divination and prophecy."

With this hypothesis as his point of departure, Nordenskiöld tabulates the numerical values on all the cords in his sixteen quipus, and comes to the following conclusions:

(1) The number 7 is used in as many combinations as possible. (The number 7, he says, is not known to have had magical significance elsewhere for the Indians of either North or South America.)

(2) Large prime numbers occur frequently, especially prime numbers with 7's in them, like 17, 37, 337, and 677. Prime numbers—1, 2, 3, 5, 7, 11, 13, 17, 19, etc.—are numbers that cannot be divided by any whole numbers other than the number 1 and themselves—numbers, that is to say, that have no whole numbers as factors or divisors. Nordenskiöld offers no suggestions as to what sort of magical significance the Indians may have attached to prime numbers. (On the symbolism of magic numbers in the Ancient World, especially among the followers of Pythagoras, see the fifth chapter of Hogben's *Mathematics for the Millions*.)

(3) Astronomical numbers are used in various combinations, especially 365 (the number of days in the solar year); 29.5 and 30 (accurate and rough calculations respectively of the lunar month); 115.9 and 116 (accurate and rough calculations respectively of the synodic period of the planet Mercury); 397 (a rough calculation of the synodic period of the planet Jupiter); and 584 (a rough calculation of the synodic period of the planet Venus). The number 52, which had calendrical significance in pre-Columbian Mexico and Yucatan (the Mayas), occurs frequently.

Nordenskiöld's analysis of his Quipu 11 (Berlin Museum für Völkerkunde V. A. 42527) exemplifies both his method and his results. This quipu has 21 pendent cords (note, he says, that 21=3 x 7), divided into four groups of 7, 4, 5, and 5 cords respectively. The values of the knots on the cords, as Nordenskiöld reads them, are as follows:

GROUP 1

1. $3285=9 \times 365$ (9 years)
2. $34167=3 \times 7 \times 1627$ (prime number)
3. $35577=1206 \times 29.5$ (1206 months)
4. $25419=3 \times 229 \times 37$ (prime numbers)
5. $37076=52 \times 713$ (prime number)
6. $20119=682 \times 29.5$ (682 months)

7.   18379=623 x 29.5+0.5 (623 months+½ day)
Total: 174022=2 x 8701 (prime number)

GROUP 2

1.   2007=5 x 365+182 (5½ solar years—½ day), or
     68 x 29.5+1 (68 months+1 day)
2.   2080=52 x 40
3.   3102=8 x 365+182 (8½ solar years—½ day)
4.   2247=3 x 7 x 107 (prime number)
Total: 9436=2 x 2 x 7 x 337 (prime number)

GROUP 3

1.   2578=2 x 1289 (prime number)
2.   2016=2 x 2 x 2 x 2 x 2 x 3 x 3 x 7
3.   3419=13 x 263 (prime numbers)
4.   3159=3 x 3 x 3 x 117 (prime number)
5.   1407=3 x 7 x 67 (prime number)
Total: 12579=1797 x 7, or 3 x 7 x 599 (prime number)

GROUP 4

1.   2178=2 x 3 x 3 x 11 x 11
2.   2085=5 x 417, or 3 x 5 x 139 (prime number)
3.   2329=17 x 137 (prime numbers)
4.   1385=5 x 277 (prime number)
5.   1501=19 x 79 (prime numbers)
Total: 9478=2 x 7 x 577 (prime number)

Nordenskiöld further notes that the sum of the numbers on the last 4 cords of Group 4 is 7300 or 20 x 365. "It can hardly be mere chance," he argues, "that of the 21 (3 x 7) numbers in the quipu one is divisible by 365, 2 by 29.5 without a remainder, 1 by 29.5 with a remainder of 0.5, 2 by 365 with a remainder of 182, which is half a year, and that the sum of the four last numbers is divisible by 365."

Do results such as these have significance? As far as the astronomical numbers are concerned, the answer seems to be that they do, and Nordenskiöld's demonstration of the way the Indians *sometimes*, in *some* quipus, concealed astronomical numbers in single cords and combinations of cords is convincing. The number 7, moreover, seems to play a conspicuous part in a few quipus, but probably not in most of them.

Prime numbers, on the other hand, do not seem to crop up with undue frequency.

Nordenskiöld attaches importance to numbers like 2578 on the first cord of Group 3, above. This number is the product of 2 and the prime number 1289. But is such a number really significant? Let us factor the next 15 numbers in sequence (i.e., 2579 to 2593), and see what kind of results we get. As might be expected, prime numbers seem to occur in the sequence as often as in the quipu itself:

$$
\begin{aligned}
2579 &= \text{(prime number)} \\
2580 &= 2 \times 2 \times 3 \times 5 \times 43 \text{ (prime number)} \\
2581 &= 29 \times 89 \text{ (prime numbers)} \\
2582 &= 2 \times 1291 \text{ (prime number)} \\
2583 &= 3 \times 3 \times 7 \times 41 \text{ (prime number)} \\
2584 &= 2 \times 2 \times 2 \times 17 \times 19 \text{ (prime numbers)} \\
2585 &= 5 \times 11 \times 47 \text{ (prime number)} \\
2586 &= 2 \times 3 \times 431 \text{ (prime number)} \\
2587 &= 13 \times 199 \text{ (prime numbers)} \\
2588 &= 2 \times 2 \times 647 \text{ (prime number)} \\
2589 &= 3 \times 863 \text{ (prime number)} \\
2590 &= 2 \times 5 \times 7 \times 37 \text{ (prime number)} \\
2591 &= \text{(prime number)} \\
2592 &= 2 \times 2 \times 2 \times 2 \times 2 \times 3 \times 3 \times 3 \times 3 \\
2593 &= \text{(prime number)}
\end{aligned}
$$

It is unlikely that the 7's and the prime numbers concealed in extant quipus have any more significance than the 7's and the prime numbers concealed in the foregoing sequence.

In 1927, two years after the appearance of Nordenskiöld's monographs, Locke published the numbers recorded on one of the quipus in the Museum of the American Indian (No. 14-3866 in the Museum's catalogue),[41] and in 1928 he published the numbers recorded on twenty-three of the quipus in the American Museum of Natural History.[42] He did not mention Nordenskiöld's hypothesis in either of these articles. Perhaps he was skeptical of its validity.

Dr. Frederick Dockstader, Director of the Museum of the American Indian, and Dr. Junius Bird, Curator of South American Archaeology in the American Museum of Natural History, kindly permitted me to examine the quipus in their collections during the summer of 1965, and

Miss Milica Dimitrijevic, a member of Dr. Bird's staff, gave me indispensable assistance in reading them. Some of the quipus examined seem to contain astronomical numbers, but none, probably, a preponderance of 7's and prime numbers. I hope to be able to publish an analysis of these quipus at a later date. For the present, in the following pages, I offer an interpretation of what I take to be (at least in part) the astronomical significance of Quipu 14-3866.

9. QUIPU 14-3866 (AN INCA ASTRONOMER'S NOTEBOOK)

Quipu 14-3866 (Museum of the American Indian) is one of the most remarkable artifacts ever salvaged from the ruins of the Inca civilization. It is a large quipu, almost complete, and unquestionably the work either of an Indian astronomer or of someone who was familiar with the results of Indian astronomical observations. Locke published it (as I have said) in 1927[43] (see facing page), but did not discuss the possible significance, magical or astronomical, of the numbers recorded on it. Had he done so, he would have discovered that it records accurate calculations of the synodic periods of Mercury, Venus, Jupiter, and the Moon. Furthermore, as I shall try to demonstrate, it records numbers and combinations of numbers which suggest that the Indian astronomer-priests of the Inca period, like the Mayas and the Stonehenge Britons, may have been able to predict the dates of lunar eclipses.

Quipu 14-3866 consists of fifteen groups of pendent cords and three individual pendent cords (lettered A to O and PQR respectively in my schematic diagram on pages 26-29). All the groups have summation cords, and all but Groups A and L have six cords each. One cord has apparently been lost from Group A, and three cords from Group L. (See the frontispiece for the way the quipu looks as currently displayed in the Museum.)

Locke thought that the quipu was unfinished. He suggested that cords P, Q, and R might have been intended as a sort of "summation group," and that if the quipu had been finished, the other groups would have been built up until the sum of their values equaled the sum of the values of P, Q, and R. He assumed that Group A had once consisted of six cords (like the other groups), and that the value of the missing cord had been 13. The sum of the numbers on the pendent cords of Group A would then have been the same—28—as the number on the summation cord. The cords in Group L probably never had any knots in them.

My view of Quipu 14-3866 differs substantially from Locke's. I accept his emendation of Group A, but I believe that in other respects the quipu is complete. It is unlikely, in my opinion, that a quipu made with such obvious care—such loving care, if you will—was put into a grave (the grave of an astronomer-priest, presumably) in an unfinished condition.

Two observations on Locke's emendation of Group A are in order here. (1) The cords in Group A are made of white cotton and dark brown cotton (mixed). Now the dark brown cotton used in a great many extant quipus has disintegrated, chemically, in the course of time; and the dark brown strands in the two-colored cords of Group A are in characteristically bad condition. It can hardly be doubted that a cord has dropped off, and that the group once contained six cords.

(2) Summation cords, for a reason that is not at all clear, do not always, in any given quipu, precisely summarize the totals registered on their respective pendent cords. Hence we cannot take it for granted that the numbers on the pendent cords of Group A of the present quipu once totaled precisely 28. However, in view of the fact that the summation cord of Group B accurately summarizes the numbers on the pendent cords of Group B, and that this total is also 28, it seems likely—almost certain, in fact—that the hypothetical missing cord in Group A had a value of 13, and that the summation cord of Group A once accurately summarized the numbers on the six original pendent cords of the group.

On this assumption, we may tabulate the values of the several groups as follows:

	Values of Knots in Pendent Cords	Values of Knots in Subsidiary Cords	Values of Knots in Summation Cords	Total Values
Group A:	28		28	56
Group B:	28		28	56
Group C:	233	34	233	500
Group D:	51		51	102
Group E:	245	32	245	522
Group F:	107	3	107	217

	Values of Knots in Pendent Cords	Values of Knots in Subsidiary Cords	Values of Knots in Summation Cords	Total Values
Group G:	25	2	25	52
Group H:	21		20	41
Group I:	59		59	118
Group J:	45		43	88
TOTALS:	842	71	839	1752

Groups K, L, M, N, O: Blank
Cord P: 245
Cord Q: 1391=12 x 115.9+0.2 (12 synodic revolutions of Mercury)
Cord R: 1159=10 x 115.9 (10 synodic revolutions of Mercury)
TOTAL: 2795

Pendent Cords A-J: 842
Subsidiary Cords A-J: 71
Summation Cords A-J: 839
TOTAL: 1752=3 x 584 (3 synodic revolutions of Venus)

White Pendent Cords   397 (1 synodic revolution of Jupiter)
White Subsidiary Cords: 23
White Summation Cords: 391
TOTAL: 811=7 x 115.9—0.3 (7 synodic revolutions of Mercury)

Brown Pendent Cords: 329
Brown Subsidiary Cords: 12
Brown Summation Cords: 329
Brown-and-White Pendent Cords: 116 (1 synodic revolution of Mercury)
Brown-and-White Subsidiary Cords: 24
Brown-and-White Summation Cords: 119
929=8 x 116+1 (8 synodic revolutions of Mercury)

Pendent Cords Group I: 59
Summation Cords Group I: 59 } 118=4 x 29.5 (4 lunations)
Pendent Cords Group J: 45
Summation Cords Group J: 43 } 88=3 x 29.5—0.5 (3 lunations)
TOTAL: 206 =7 x 29.5—0.5 (7 lunations)

MUSEUM OF THE AMERICAN INDIAN HEYE FOUNDATION
QUIPU 14/3866 (ICA) SCHEMATIC DIAGRAM

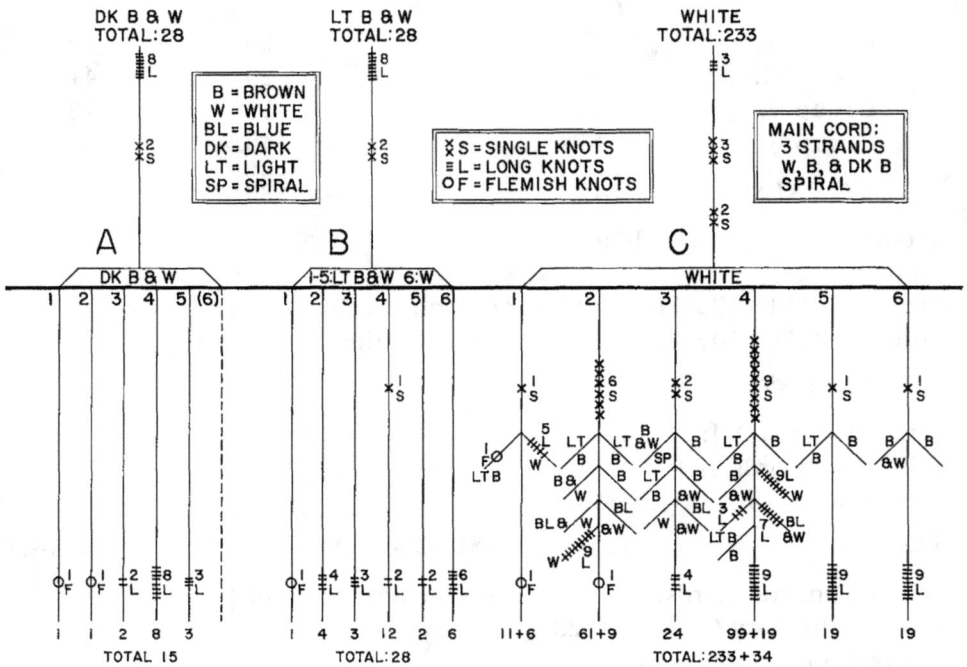

DK B & W TOTAL: 28   LT B & W TOTAL: 28   WHITE TOTAL: 233

B = BROWN
W = WHITE
BL = BLUE
DK = DARK
LT = LIGHT
SP = SPIRAL

S = SINGLE KNOTS
L = LONG KNOTS
F = FLEMISH KNOTS

MAIN CORD:
3 STRANDS
W, B, & DK B
SPIRAL

A   B   C

DK B & W   1-5:LT B&W 6:W   WHITE

TOTAL 15   TOTAL: 28   TOTAL: 233 + 34

Cord Q: 1391

Cord R: 1159

TOTAL: 2550=85 x 30 (85 lunations of 30 days each)

Pendent Cords A-J: 842

Subsidiary Cords A-J: 71

TOTAL: 913=2 x 365+183 (2½ years)

Brown, White, and Brown-and-White Subsidiary Cords: 59=2 x 29. 5 (2 lunations)

All Cords in Groups A-J except the Blue and the Blue-and-White Subsidiary Cords: 1740=15 x 116 (15 synodic periods of Mercury)

The foregoing astronomical numbers are too precise and too numerous, it would seem, to be the result of chance. The Indian astronomers of Peru may, after all, have been very nearly as competent as their more celebrated Maya contemporaries.

QUIPU 14/3866 (CONTINUED)

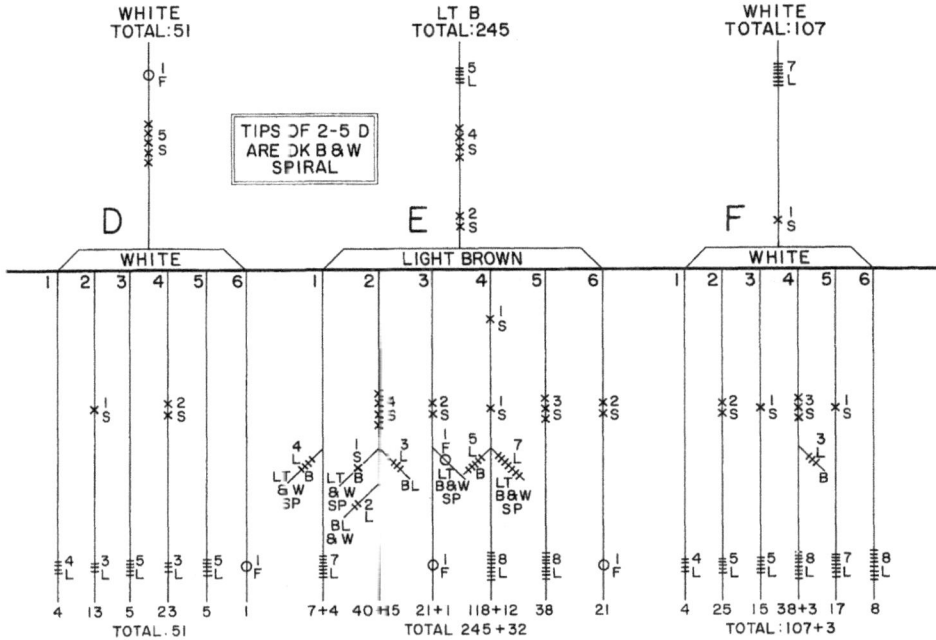

WHITE TOTAL:51 LT B TOTAL:245 WHITE TOTAL:107

TIPS OF 2-5 D ARE DK B & W SPIRAL

D   WHITE

E   LIGHT BROWN

F   WHITE

TOTAL:51   TOTAL 245+32   TOTAL:107+3

If they were, they could probably, like the Mayas, predict the dates of eclipses. They had observation towers, four to the east of Cuzco, and four to the west, less impressive, no doubt, than the magnificent Maya observatory at Chichen Itza, but perfectly aligned, according to Garcilaso, for observations of the Sun (and of the Moon, too, of course, though Garcilaso does not specifically say so).

The Incas claimed descent from the Sun and the Moon, built temples in honor of the Sun and the Moon, and worshiped the Sun and the Moon. The Inca astronomer-priests, we may be sure, kept track (on quipus) of solstices, equinoxes, azimuths, declinations, and eclipses with pious as well as scientific zeal. From their point of view, furthermore, nothing could have been more conducive to the perpetuation of their priestly power than the announcement of a potentially catastrophic phenomenon like an eclipse, and then, when the dread event occurred, the nullification of its consequences by the beating of drums,

QUIPU 14 3866 (CONTINUED)

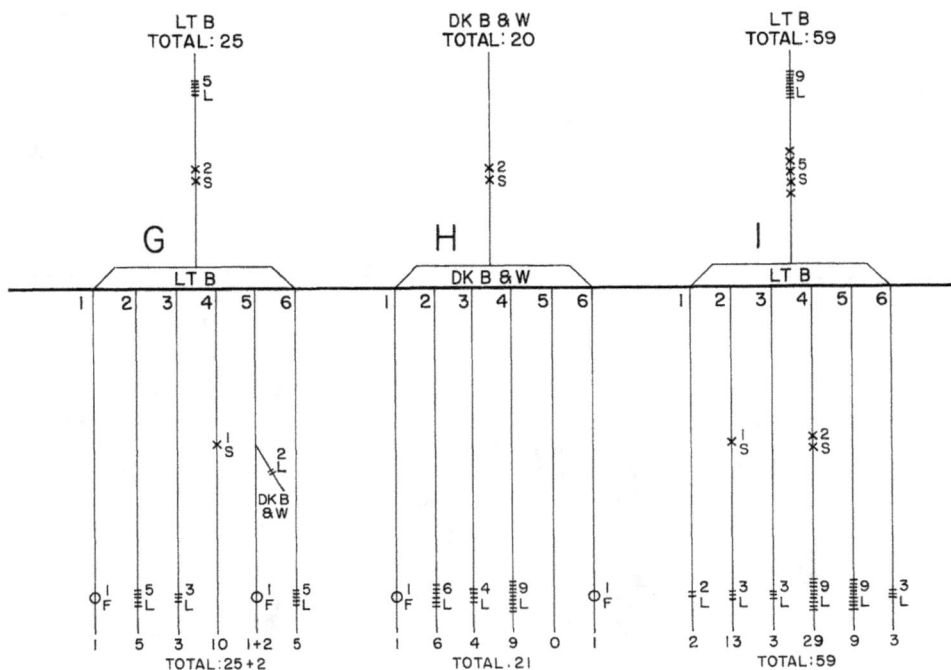

the blowing of trumpets, and other traditional expedients of the sort described by Garcilaso.

Quipu 14-3866 may, conceivably, contain information about eclipses. The number 52, Nordenskiöld notes, often occurs in the quipus he studied, and the number 52 in the Maya calendar signified the sacred 52-year period which archaeologists call the Calendar Round. The Aztecs borrowed it from the Mayas, and perhaps the Peruvian Indians did too. "It is difficult to imagine," says Nordenskiöld, "there being no connexion between their astronomical knowledge and that of the Maya stock."[44] The number 52, in other words, may sometimes represent years rather than days when tied in calendrical quipus. Perhaps it does in Group G of Quipu 14-3866 (25+25+2=52).

Other numbers in quipus, therefore, may also represent years. Four possibilities in Quipu 14-3866 are: 56 (the sum of the numbers on each of the first two groups); 1681 (the sum of the numbers on all pendent

QUIPU 14/3866 (CONCLUDED)

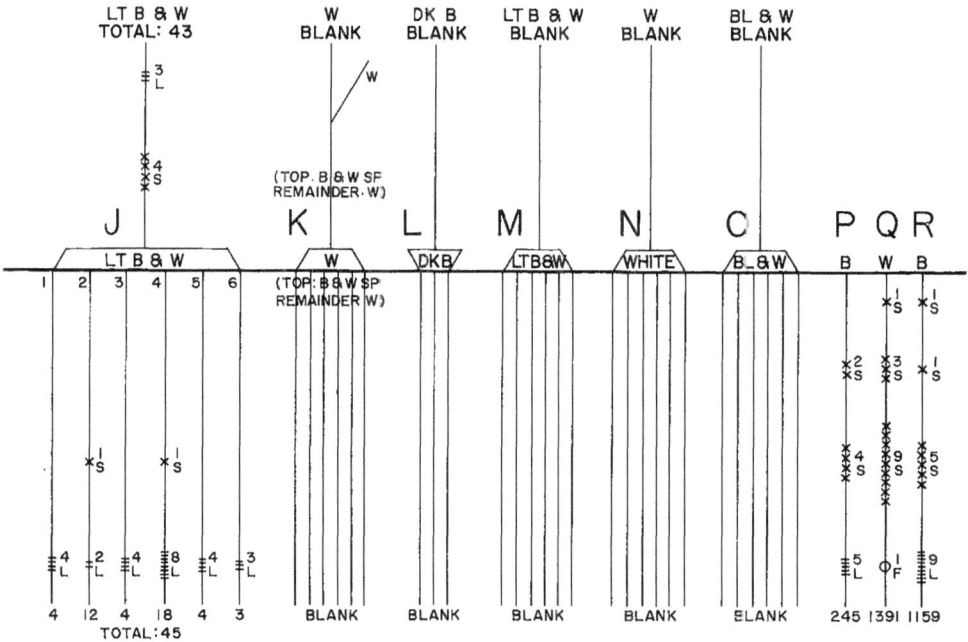

LT B & W TOTAL: 43	W BLANK	DK B BLANK	LT B & W BLANK	W BLANK	BL & W BLANK

(TOP. B &W SP REMAINDER· W)

J   K   L   M   N   O   P Q R

LT B & W	W	DKB	LTB&W	WHITE	B & W	B	W	B

(TOP: B&W SP REMAINDER W)

4	12	4	18	4	3	BLANK	BLANK	BLANK	BLANK	BLANK	245	391	159

TOTAL: 45

and summation cords in Groups A-J); 670 (the sum of the numbers on all brown cords in Group A-J); and 2795 (the sum of the numbers on cords PQR).

Gerald Hawkins in his provocative book on the use of Stonehenge as an astronomical observatory[45] shows that the number 56, representing a period of 56 years, governs the cyclical pattern of seasonal eclipses. The interval between identical eclipses, he notes, is approximately but not exactly 19 years. Since a rigid 19-year cycle is inaccurate, a correction has to be made (and apparently *was* made at Stonehenge) every 56 years; and so the pattern of eclipses becomes (more or less irregularly) 19+19+18, and so on, with about two periods of 19 years for every one period of 18 years.

This cycle, which Hawkins calls the Stonehenge cycle, averages about 18.67 years. It keeps in step, therefore, with the Moon, since the "regression of the nodes of the Moon's orbit is 18.61 years." Moreover,

Hawkins points out, "it keeps in step with eclipses becaues the metonic cycle of 19 years and the saros of 18 years are both eclipse cycles. The metonic cycle has not been previously recognized as an eclipse cycle, probably because it runs for only 57 years or so. It is, however, a remarkable cycle, because eclipses repeat on the same calendar date. The lunar eclipse of December 19, 1964, for example, follows the lunar eclipse of December 19, 1945."[46]

The number 56 is registered on each of the first two groups of cords in Quipu 14-3866. The number 1681 is the sum of 60 x 19 and 30 x 18 (plus 1), or a ratio of two 19's to one 18. Or, to use the Stonehenge cycle in calculating the result, 18.67 x 90=1680.3, or 0.7 of a year less than 1681 years. The number 670 is the sum of 23 x 19 and 13 x 18 (minus 1). Or 18.62 x 36=670.32. The number 2795=18.63 x 150 plus 0.5.

Did the Peruvian Indians, observing the Sun and the Moon for several hundred years, come to the same conclusions as the hypothetical Hyperboreans of Stonehenge? Quipu 14-3866, I am afraid, *proves* nothing. But it points the way to a possible line of inquiry in future studies of the quipu. And if it is an eclipse quipu, as it almost certainly is a Venus, Jupiter, and Mercury quipu, the apparently meaningless 245 on Cord P, side by side with the meaningful 1391 and 1159 on Cords P and Q, is seen to have a *raison d'être*; i.e., 245 plus 1391 plus 1159 equals 2795 or almost exactly 150 of Hawkins's Stonehenge cycles.

Garcilaso and Huaman Poma, half Incas both, were aware that the Indian astrologers (as they called the astronomer-priests) were interested in eclipses. Garcilaso belittles their knowledge of astronomy, but admits that they "knew about the different eclipses," the solstices, the equinoxes, and the apparent movements of the Sun, the Moon, and the planet Venus. They "simply did not see" the other planets, he mistakenly asserts. Their purpose in observing the solstices and the equinoxes, he says, was to regulate the calendar and to fix the proper times to sow and harvest the crops.[47]

Huaman Poma, a less intelligent observer than Garcilaso, says that the astrologers knew about the stars, the comets, the course of the Sun from summer to winter, the phases of the Moon, the eclipses of the Moon ("el clipsar de la luna"—lines 8-9, page 885 of his manuscript), and the hours, days, weeks, months, and years. Like Garcilaso, he stresses the fact that the astrologers fixed the dates for sowing and harvesting the crops and for celebrating the festivals of the Sun. The astrologer he depicts on page 883 of his manuscript (see page 34, below) was a hundred and fifty years old, he says, had good eyes, ate as well as a young man, and had never lost a tooth. The Sun according to Huaman Poma, had a beard which could be plucked like the beard of a man.[48]

Garcilaso and Huaman Poma, though of royal descent, were to all intents and purposes outsiders. We must remember, when we evaluate their accounts of Peruvian astronomy, that they would not have had an opportunity to learn the more esoteric secrets of the priestly caste. It is all the more significant, therefore, that both of them mention the astrologers' knowledge of eclipses.

The manuscript of Huaman Poma's *Nueva Corónica*, discovered in the Royal Danish Library in 1908, has clarified many previously obscure aspects of life in pre-Spanish Peru. The author, like Garcilaso "el Inca," was the son of a Spanish father and an Indian mother, and like Garcilaso he eventually went to Spain and wrote a book. His purpose (in part) was to call attention to the cruelty of the Spaniards to his mother's people.

A facsimile of his manuscript was published in Paris in 1936, and a modern Spanish translation (the first half of the book only) in Lima in 1956. The drawings on the following pages are reproduced by the kind permission of the Danish National Librarian, Mr. Palle Birkelund. Three of them illustrate the skill of the Indians in the use of cordage (weaving and bridge building); one depicts a *chasqui* or relay runner; and the remainder depict officials holding quipus.

10. The Inca Abacus

The last drawing by Huaman Poma on page 35, below, depicts the Inca's treasurer holding a large unknotted quipu, and in the corner of the drawing there is a rectangle divided into twenty squares containing, in a systematic arrangement, a number of small circles and dots.

Henry Wassén suggested in 1931 that the rectangle in the drawing represents a counting board or abacus which the Indians used to "work out computations the results of which were subsequently recorded by knots on the cords of the quipus."[49] The little circles in the squares, he surmised, represent empty holes, and the dots represent holes that have been filled by pebbles or grains of maize.

In support of this ingenious conjecture, Wassén quotes Father José de Acosta, who lived in Peru from 1571 to 1586 and published a book entitled *Historia Natural y Moral de las Indias* in 1596:

> To see them use another kind of quipu with maize kernels is a perfect joy. In order to effect a very difficult computation for which an able calculator would require pen and ink for the various methods of calculation these Indians make use of their kernels. They place one here, three somewhere else and eight I know not where. They move one kernel here and three there and the fact is that they are able to complete their computation without making the smallest mistake. As a matter of fact, they are better at calculating what each one is due to pay or give than we should be with pen and ink. Whether

---

HUAMAN POMA DE AYALA

Page 33:
1. Before the Conquest: A thirty-three-year-old woman with a typical backstrap loom.
2. After the Conquest: A woman weaving with the tears running down her face.
3. The inspector of bridges and a rope bridge.
4. A post-Conquest official holding both a quipu and a book.

Page 34:
1. The custodian of the imperial storehouses reporting to the Inca Topa Yupanqui (1471-1493).
2. The imperial secretary.
3. A provincial administrator.
4. A venerable astrologer and philosopher.

Page 35:
1. An eighteen-year-old village messenger.
2. A *chasqui* or relay runner with a white cap, blowing a conch shell horn to warn of his approach, and carrying a club, a sling, and a bag—the bag, perhaps, containing a quipu.
3. The imperial treasurer with counting board or abacus.
4. Wassén's suggested values for the squares in the counting board.

POMA DE AYALA C. 1600

PRIMERA CALLE
AVACOCVARMI

645

FRAILE.DOMINICOMVI.

GOVERNADOR.DELOS.PVENTES.DESTER.
CHACASVIOIOCACOSIVGA
GVAMBOCHACA

350

REGIDORES
TENGA.LIBRO.QVIPO.CV

800

33

POMA DE AYALA C. 1600

POMA DE AYALA C. 1600

QVITO CALLE
SAIA PAIAC 20

COREON·MAIOR·IMENOR
HATVNCHASQVICHVRV
MVLLO·CHASQVI·CVRACA~ 35

CŌTADOR·MAIOR·ITEZORERO 360
TAVANTINSVIOQVIPOC
CVRACA·CON DOR·CHAVA

WASSÉN'S SOLUTION 1931

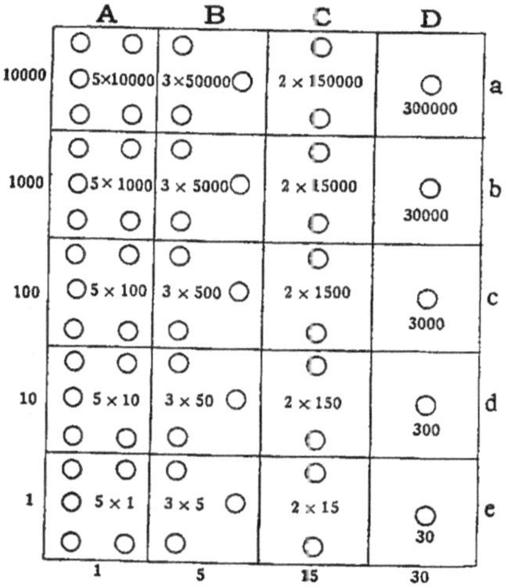

	A	B	C	D	
10000	5×10000	3×50000	2×150000	300000	a
1000	5×1000	3×5000	2×15000	30000	b
100	5×100	3×500	2×1500	3000	c
10	5×10	3×50	2×150	300	d
1	5×1	3×5	2×15	30	e
	1	5	15	30	

this is not ingenious and whether these people are wild animals let those judge who will! What I consider as certain is that in what they undertake to do they are superior to us.

Father Acosta might almost be describing the manipulation of the buttons on the rods of an oriental abacus. Other early chroniclers, quoted by Wassén in an expanded version of his article,[50] mention the use of pebbles as well as grains of maize for mathematical computations. Wassén is on firm ground, it would seem, in his assumption that Huaman Poma's rectangle represents a counting board.

THE INCA ABACUS

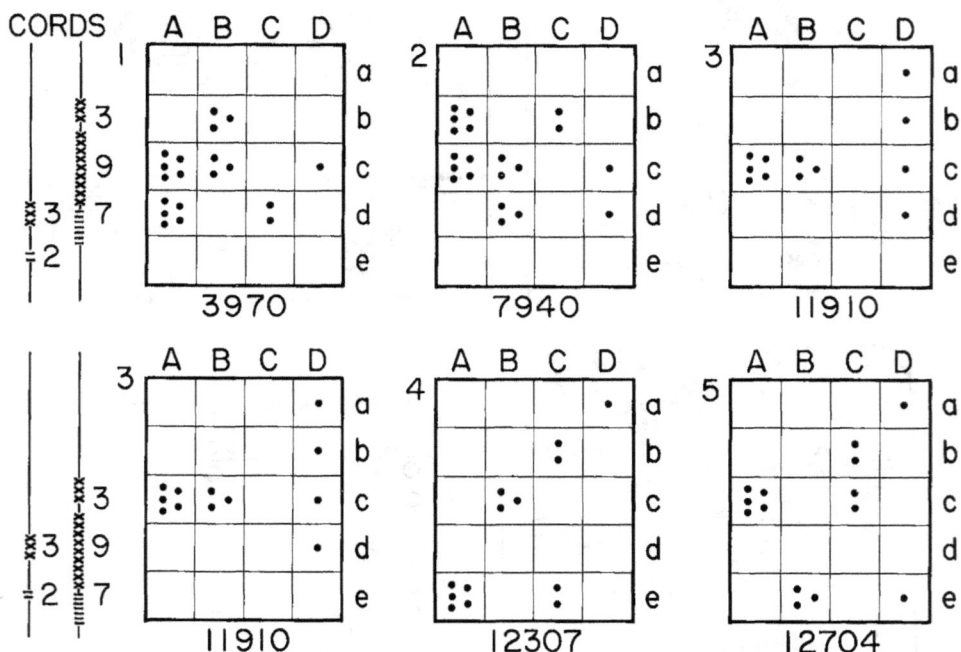

CORDS

1   A B C D   a b c d e   3970

2   A B C D   a b c d e   7940

3   A B C D   a b c d e   11910

3   A B C D   a b c d e   11910

4   A B C D   a b c d e   12307

5   A B C D   a b c d e   12704

The way he thinks the counting board may have been used, however, is open to question. Of his diagram (see page 35), he says:

We see that the plate is provided with two sets of coordinates. Of these the vertical ones, e.g. row *A*, operate in accordance with the method by which the decimal system is used in quipu computation and thus directly corresponds to an individual quipu cord in which the knots indicating units are at the bottom, the tens next above them, and so on. By reason of the vertical rows each consisting of five squares, all the numbers contained in the horizontal row *a* become multiples of 10,000.

In regard to the numerical values represented by the horizontal rows, they are based on the important part that the number 5, i.e. a hand, plays among many peoples, and evidently also in the past has played in the development of the decimal system in Peru. Thus, in the holes found in the square *Ae*, a number of stones, say 3, may be placed in symbolization of the number 3 of a certain unit. Should it be required to mark a further three units the square would be overfilled, wherefore one of the holes in the square *Be* is at once made to substitute five of the units of the square *Ae*, and so on. The example just given is purposely made extremely simple.

Two mathematicians whom I have consulted have read Wassén's article, and both (if I understand their analyses correctly) regard his suggested way of using the counting board as possible but unlikely. Gordon Walker, Executive Director of the American Mathematical Society, writes that it cannot be accepted "unless there is other evidence to substantiate the special role of 5, 15, and 30 in Peruvian arithmetic." Robert Jackson, Professor of Mathematics in the University of Toledo, objects to the assumption of "a positional notation within the horizontal row employing three bases other than decimal, i.e. binary, ternary, and quinary." The multiples of three, he writes, are "inconsistent with proper decimal positional notation" and "distinctly unnatural." He calls particular attention to Huaman Poma's reference to the figure 100,000 in the following passage:

"*Hatun Hucha Quipoc,* the chief accountant, and *Uchuy Hucha Quipoc,* the lesser accountant, kept their accounts just as one does with a calculating table, counting from a hundred thousand, ten thousand, hundred, ten, down to one. With this system they could determine and count everything that happened in the kingdom."[51]

Professor Jackson remarks that the pebbles would presumably have been placed in the holes in such a way as to make for the quickest and easiest possible recognition of the digits represented. To multiply two numbers on the board—32, say, and 397 (the synodic period of Jupiter) —he suggests the following procedure:

First, align the board with two cords in which knots denoting the numbers 32 and 397 have been tied. (See Inca abacas diagrams on page

36.) Next, register the number 3970 (397 x 10) on the board by placing pebbles in the holes as shown in Figure 1. Add a second 3970 to the first, as shown in Figure 2, and a third to the sum of the first two, as shown in Figure 3. To do this, begin by adding 7 pebbles to the 7 already placed in horizontal row d. Since the first 2 of these additional 7 pebbles will bring the count in row d to 9, remove all pebbles from row d and add 1 pebble (value: 10) to row c. Place the remaining 4 pebbles in row d. Proceed in the same manner with the digits 9 and 3 in horizontal rows c and b. Finally, add two 397's to the product 11910 (397 x 30), as shown in Figures 4 and 5.

The product, 12704, can be readily transferred from board to quipu. The chance of error is minimal because the horizontal rows on quipu and board correspond. Of course, the Indians may not have used the board in precisely this way, or even a board of precisely this design. One thing, however, is certain: quipus alone, as Locke and Wassén insist, are not adapted to arithmetical computation.

11. STATISTICAL AND CULTURAL QUIPUS

Locke, in a review of Wassén's article,[52] suggested that the last major discovery concerning the quipu had probably been made. It may be so. Certainly, at this late date, we are unlikely to recover any of the statistical and cultural quipus that were on file at the royal "library" in Cuzco at the time of the Spanish conquest, and even if one or two should turn up, we would be unable to read and interpret them.

Statistical quipus, the chroniclers tell us, contained detailed records and accounts of all the material resources of the Inca empire. Garcilaso describes the census records, for example, as follows:

> In order to ascertain the number of vassals in the Empire, they started with each village, then with each province: the first cord showed a census of men over sixty, the second, those between fifty and sixty, the third, those from forty to fifty, and so on, by decades, down to the babes at the breast.
> Occasionally other, thinner, cords of the same color, could be seen among one of these series, as though they represented an exception to the rule; thus, for instance, among the figures that concerned the men of such and such an age, all of whom were considered to be

married, the thinner cords indicated the number of widowers of the same age, for the year in question: because, as I explained before, population figures, together with those of all the other resources of the Empire, were brought up to date every year.[53]

The resources that were catalogued in this way included crops and agricultural produce, herds of domestic and wild animals, stores of wool and cotton, weapons and other military supplies—everything in the empire, in fact, that could be counted. Material things were listed according to categories analogous to the ten-year age-groups of the census reports. An inventory of the weapons of the army, for example, would begin with the most important, the lances (registered, presumably, on the first cord or group of cords of the quipu), and proceed to the javelins, the bows and arrows, the hatchets, the clubs, and the slings.

Storage huts for emergency rations and other military supplies were erected at strategic locations throughout the empire, and their contents were listed on quipus. One of Huaman Poma's drawings (see page 34) shows a *quipucamayu* or quipu-keeper, quipu in hand, standing beside some thatched-roofed storage huts and making a report to the Inca Topa Yupanqui.

Four *quipucamayus* were assigned to the smaller villages of the empire, and as many as twenty or thirty to the larger ones. Trained runners called *chasquis* were stationed in pairs at intervals of about a mile along the imperial highways. Running at top speed and handing their quipus on, one *chasqui* to another, as in a relay race, they could transmit a message to Cuzco from two or three hundred miles away in twenty-four hours. One of Huaman Poma's drawings of a *chasqui* is reproduced on page 35.

The cultural quipus mentioned by the Spanish chroniclers "recorded" laws, rites, treaties, speeches, and history. No specimens seem to have survived, and so we may never know what improvements the ingenious Peruvian Indians made in them as compared with the knot-records of, say, the Marquesas Islands. The *quipucamayus* who had charge of them and served as the official historians of the empire evidently relied on the usual psychological expedients—association, interest, concentration, and repetition—in order to fix the facts in their memories. They never "let their quipus out of their hands," says Garcilaso, "and they kept passing their cords and knots through their fingers so as not to forget the tradition" which it was their function to remember.[54]

The sacred Calendar Round of 52 years in pre-Spanish Mexico was called *xiuh-molpilli,* which meant, literally, "knotted years," and in Mapa de Tepechpan the first year of the period was always indicated by a knot. "If the Mexicans had quipus like the Peruvians," observes Nordenskiöld, "we are right in trying to trace them to a common origin."[55] The point is well taken: and the common origin, we can be reasonably sure, was the universal, indispensable, primordial knot-calendar.

Chapter Two: Magic Knots

1. HOMEOPATHIC AND CONTAGIOUS MAGIC

WHEN MACBETH, in Shakespeare's tragedy, exhorts the witches to unlock the secrets of his fate, even if they have to "untie the winds" and set them free to "swallow navigation up," he is speaking literally, not metaphorically: he means precisely what he says. For flesh-and-blood witches in Shakespeare's day sold wind-knots to mariners in many English and Continental ports, and a majority of the members of Shakespeare's audiences, like Macbeth himself, believed—we cannot doubt it —that witches could imprison the wind in knotted strings and handkerchiefs.

And when Robert Burns, in his "Address to the Deil," warns his readers to beware of the "mystic knots" that "make great abuse" on young married men by rendering them sexually impotent, he is speaking of the dread *Nestelknüpfen* or *ligaturae,* outlawed by Church and State, yet still being tied in Scotland, among other places, at the end of the Age of Enlightenment and Reason. Primitive and unsophisticated people everywhere and in every age have believed in the magic power, for good or evil, of knots.

It is difficult for us in the scientifically oriented twentieth century to understand how it was ever possible for anybody, no matter how primitive and unsophisticated, to believe in magic, for magic violates what we have become accustomed to thinking of as the self-evident laws of natural cause and effect. We must remember, however, that primitive man did not view the universe in the same way we do. He thought of the universe as something sentient and alive. The Sun and the Moon, for primitive man, were deities; disease and death were the work of devils; and he took it for granted that a mysterious spiritual power which anthropologists call *mana* (a Polynesian word) animates all

41

things both material and immaterial. Primitive man, reasoning from such premises, may be pardoned for believing in what he would have called, perhaps—if he had been given to conscious metaphysical analysis —the self-evident laws of *extra*-natural cause and effect.

Magic does, indeed, seem to function in accordance with more or less systematic laws. Tylor calls it a systematic pseudo-science based on a fallacious association of ideas. Frazer calls it the precursor of religion. Magic, he says, seeks to coerce the supernatural; religion seeks to propitiate it. Marett, Hubert, and Preuss stress the dynamic role in magic of *mana*.[1]

Frazer distinguishes two kinds of magic: homeopathic (or imitative) and contagious. Both kinds conform to what he calls the Law of Sympathy, or the Law that "like produces like." Things act on each other, even at a distance, according to this Law, (1) if they are alike in some relevant respect, or (2) if they were formerly joined or in contact with each other. The first of these conditions obtains in homeopathic magic, the second in contagious magic.

Sticking pins into a waxen image of an enemy in order to hurt or kill him is an example of homeopathic magic. So also is the use of bear grease as a cure for baldness; for like produces like, according to the Law of Sympathy, and bears are very hairy animals. Contagious magic is illustrated by the belief that it is possible to gain power over an enemy by getting hold of a lock of his hair or a piece of his clothing. For this reason the hair clippings, the nail parings, and even the spittle of primitive chieftains were sometimes scrupulously protected lest they be stolen and put to harmful magic use.

The importance of knots in magic is due in part to the symbolic relationship between their function as a useful tool (to bind and to tie) and the constraint that magic in general imposes, so primitive people believe, on all sorts of natural and supernatural phenomena. "The ancients," says Kirby Smith, "habitually associated the processes of magic with the ideas of binding, tying up, nailing down, and their opposites. A magic act is a κατάδεσμος, a κατάδεσις, a *defixio*, a *devinctio*; the removal of its effect is an ἀνάλυσις, a *solutio*." "The primary object and supposed result of every charm," he remarks, "is some form of restraint."[2]

"The act of tying a knot," says Dilling, "implies something 'bound,' and hence the action becomes a spell towards hindering the actions of other persons or things. Similarly, the act of loosing a knot implies the removal of the impediment caused by the knot, and from this belief are derived the various customs of unloosing knots, unlocking and opening doors and cupboards, and setting free captive animals at any period when undesirable hindrance of any event is feared."[3]

Magic knots exemplify the principles of homeopathic magic. They are presumed (by primitive people) to have power over the following phenomena: (1) the weather; (2) disease and death; (3) sex (including love, marriage, conception, and childbirth); and (4) spirits, demons, and deities. These categories are not mutually exclusive, and instances are found that do not fit into any of them.

The influence of magic knots may be: (1) either maleficent or beneficent; (2) either intentional or spontaneous; (3) effective either at close range or at a distance; (4) effective either at once or after a lapse of time; and (5) the work either of a layman or of a professional (a witch, a wizard, or a medicine man).

When the influence is intentional—that is, when it is consciously directed by the person who ties the knot—the knot may be tied either in silence or in conjunction with the utterance of a magic spell. Blowing or spitting on a magic knot is sometimes supposed to increase its power. A beneficent knot may be either actively beneficent or passively apotropaic (protective).

2. WIND AND RAIN

Rain makers and wind brokers flourish in primitive communities where survival depends on the amount of rainfall and the strength and direction of the wind.

Rain makers rely on homeopathic rituals like dripping water down through the leaves of trees in imitation of rain, and blowing water out of the mouth through the lips in imitation of mist. They do not use knots, because knots inhibit and restrain, and would cause the rain to stop rather than to make it fall. In northern India, for example, where there is apt to be too much rain, the inhabitants of Mirzapur "name twenty-one men who are blind of an eye, tie twenty-one knots in a cord, and fix it under the eaves of the house in order to bind the rain."[4]

Wind brokers profess to be able to bind the wind with knots so that it can be carried aboard a ship for use during a voyage. Thus in the *Odyssey* (to cite what is probably the earliest allusion in literature to wind-knots), Æolus, king of the winds, gives Ulysses a bag with all the winds except the west wind tied up in it by means of a silver cord. After a favorable voyage of nine days, Ulysses falls asleep at the helm, and his men open the bag in order to share the treasure they imagine it contains. The conflicting winds burst forth, and the ship, though in sight of Ithaca, is driven back to Æolus's magic island.[5]

Wind-knots reappear in literature in the fourth century A. D. During the reign of Constantine the Great, a man by the name of Sopater was put to death in Constantinople "on a charge of binding the winds by magic, because it happened that the corn-ships of Egypt and Syria were detained afar off by calms or head winds, to the rage and disappointment of the hungry Byzantine rabble."[6]

During the Middle Ages, and even as late as the present century, a considerable traffic in wind-knots was carried on in the seaports of Finland, Lapland, Denmark, Ireland, Shetland, the Orkneys, the Hebrides, the Isle of Man, and elsewhere. "In that ilond [the Isle of Man]," wrote Ranulf Higden in the fourteenth century, "is sortilege and wicchecraft i-vsed. For wommen there sellith to schipmen wynde, as it were i-closed vnder thre knottes of threde, so that the more wynd he wol haue, he wil vnknette the mo knottes."[7]

The wind brokers of the North, unlike Æolus, usually tried to control the strength of the wind rather than its direction. Thomas Nash, however, one of Shakespeare's contemporaries, asserts that the witches of Ireland and Denmark will sell a man a wind that will "blow him safe unto what coast he will."[8] Three knots in a thread, he says, or an old "grandams blessing in the corner of a napkin, will carry you all the world over." When a man frowns, Nash remarks, he knits his brows; but "let a wizard knit a noose . . . & it is haile, storm, and tempest a month after."[9]

The witches and wizards of Finland and Lapland were especially celebrated as wind brokers. Olaus Magnus, writing in 1555, has this to say about them:

> The *Finlanders* were wont formerly amongst their other Errors of Gentilisme, to sell Wines to Merchants, that were stopt on their

Coasts by contrary Weather and when they had their price, they knit three Magical knots, not like to the Laws of *Cassius,* bound up with a Thong, and they gave them unto the Merchants; observing that rule, that when they unloosed the first, they should have a good Gale of Wind: when the second, a stronger wind: but when they untied the third, they should have such cruel Tempests, that they should not be able to look out of the Forecastle to avoid the Rocks, nor move a foot to pull down the Sails, nor stand at the Helm to govern the ship; and they made an unhappy trial of the truth of it, who denied that there was any such power in those knots.[10]

An ancient Norse myth tells how the lame smith Volundr, whose father was a Finnish king, had a supply of wind-knots in his smithy. "A long rope of bast hung there, with knots in it at regular intervals. In each and every knot a storm wind was bound. Each week he untied a knot and freed the wind that was bound in it, and sent it south with his mad song, charged with clouds and hail."[11]

The Laplanders, according to Giles Fletcher (1588), give their friends good winds, and "contrary to other, whom they meane to hurt, by tying of certaine knots vpon a rope (somewhat like to the tale of Æolus his windbag)."[12] And Knud Leems, in his account of the Lap-landers (1767), tells of a Lapland witch who confessed that she and three other witches had assumed the forms of birds (an eagle, a swan, a crow, and a dove), put to sea in a tub, and destroyed a ship by invoking the devil and untying knots.[13]

Richard Eden (1555) says that the Lapps were expert enchanters. "They tye three knottes on a strynge," he says, and when they "lose" one, "they rayse tollerable wyndes. When they lose an other, the wynde is more vehement. But by losyng the thyrde, they rayse playne tempestes."[14]

Peder Claussøn Friis (1545-1614) writes that a Lapp who lived in Norway claimed to be able to raise any wind he wanted, especially the wind that was blowing when he was born. He sold the usual three knots to mariners, and advised them to use the second knot. Untying the third knot, he said, would result in shipwreck and loss of life.[15]

The peasants of Esthonia used to blame the witches of Finland for the bitter northeast winds that sweep down in the spring across the

Gulf of Finland, "bringing ague and rheumatic inflammations in their train."[16] An Esthonian song, quoted by Frazer, runs as follows:

> Wind of the Cross! rushing and mighty!
> Heavy the blow of thy wings sweeping past!
> Wild wailing winds of misfortune and sorrow,
> Wizards of Finland ride by on the blast.[17]

The witches of *Macbeth,* as befits their Northern character, have power over the wind:

> 2 [Witch]. Ile give thee a Winde.
> 1. Th' art kinde.
> 3. And I another.
> 1. I myself have all the other;
> And the very ports they blow,
> All the quarters that they know
> I' th' shipman's card.

And so, equipped with the winds she needs, the first witch proposes to sail to Aleppo in a sieve in order to wreak vengeance on the master of the *Tiger,* whose wife (a "rump-fed ronyon," in her opinion) has insulted her.

> 1. Though his bark cannot be lost,
> Yet it shall be tempest-tost.—
> Look what I have.
> 2. Show me, show me.
> 1. Here I have a pilot's thumb,
> Wrackt as homeward he did come.

Shakespeare, like Homer and the unknown Esthonian bard whose verses are quoted above, wrings poetry from the superstition.

3. SICKNESS AND DISEASE

The belief that magic knots can cure all kinds of ills is common in every age and in all parts of the world. In Babylonia and Assyria, as we know from a number of cuneiform tablets dating from the eighth century B. C., knots were used to cure headaches and other ailments. The following prescription is from Tablet IX in the British Museum:

Take cedar . . . and
Plait a triple cord . . and
Tie twice seven knots and
Perform the Incantation of Eridu and
Bind the head of the sick man,
That the evil Spirit, the evil Demon, may stand aside,
And a kindly Spirit, a kindly Genius be present.[18]

This prescription is interesting for a number of reasons, and in particular because the knots are tied in the plaited bark of a tree. In magic, once a rite or formula is established, it tends to remain fixed and unaltered even after the original reasons for some of the details have been forgotten. Since the Babylonians and Assyrians were capable spinners and weavers, it is conceivable that the use of bark instead of woolen cords in the present rite may have been the vestige of a tradition that had been established before spinning was invented, when only the crudest sort of cordage was as yet available.

We have here, therefore, a clue to the antiquity of magic knots. "We are justified in assuming," says Thompson, referring to the prescriptions of which the one quoted above is an example, "that we have in our hands at the present time tolerably accurate copies of the exorcisms and spells which the Sumerian and his Babylonian successor employed some six or seven thousand years ago, to avert the attacks of devils, and to ward off malign influences of every kind."[19] This, I suggest, is a conservative estimate of the age of magic knots.

The prescription quoted above does not provide any hints as to how the knots were supposed to effect the removal of the headache. Another prescription, however, indicates that the evil was thought to be bound by the knots, as if it were a tangible object, so that it could be removed to a distant place and disposed of:

He hath turned his [steps?] to a Temple-woman (?),
Istar hath sent her Temple-woman (?),
Hath seated the wise woman on a couch,
That she may spin white and black wool into a double cord,
A strong cord, a mighty cord, a twi-colored cord on a spindle,
A cord to overcome the Ban:
Against the evil curse of human Ban,
Against a divine curse,

A cord to overcome the Ban.
He hath bound it on the head,
On the hand and foot of this man,
Marduk, the son of Eridu, the Prince,
With his undefiled hands cutteth it off,
That the Ban—its cord—
May go forth to the desert, to a clean place,
That the evil Ban may stand aside,
And this man may be clean and undefiled,
Into the favouring hands of his god may he be commended.[20]

Knots in which sickness is thought to be bound are often thrown into running water. In modern Rumania a woman reputed to be a sorceress used the following prescription to cure a man of lumbago. Laying her hands obliquely across the man's back, she tied nine knots in a hempen cord, and as she tied each knot she uttered one of the following charms:

"1. I do not bind the knot, but the pain in the heart. 2. I do not bind the knot, but the pain in the intestines. 3. I do not bind the knot, but the pain in the liver. And so on 4. for the ribs, 5. for the shoulders, 6. for the breast, 7. for the throat, 8. for the neck, ears, and teeth, 9. for all the joints and all the other parts of the body."[21]

The sorceress then put the cord into a pitcher of water, uttered another charm, laid the cord crosswise on the patient's breast, and left it there three days. Then she threw the cord with its knots into running water—not into a well, for fear that if she did so, the people who drank from the well would also get lumbago.

Another way to get rid of an illness was to tie it to a tree. In nineteenth-century Germany, a peasant who had a fever would attach a straw to the trunk of a tree and utter certain charms, and the tree, he thought, would contract the fever. Or, according to another variation of the formula, he would wrap a blue woolen thread nine times round a toe of his left foot, wear it for several days, go before sunset to an elder bush, tie a knot in it, and say: "Good evening, Mr. Elder, here I bring my fever; I tie it to you and go on my way."[22]

In Holland, a peasant with a cold would go to a willow tree, tie three knots in a branch, and say: "Good morning, old fellow, I give you my cold, good morning, old fellow." In New England, a cure for the

48

ague was to tie the left hand loosely to an apple tree with a string made of three-colored woolen yarn, slip the hand quickly out of the knot, and run home without looking back.[23]

Frazer cites numerous instances from England and the Continent of the belief that gout, warts, fever, and other ills can be transferred to trees, either by means of knots, or in some other way. The "still, sad music of humanity" is audible in Frazer's description of the following practice:

"Not far from Marburg, at a place called Neuhof, there is a wood of birches. Thither on a morning before sunrise, in the last quarter of the moon, bands of gouty people may often be seen hobbling in silence. Each of them takes his stand before a separate tree and pronounces these solemn words: 'Here stand I before the judgment bar of God and tie up all my gout. All the disease in my body shall remain tied up in this birch-tree.' Meanwhile the good physician ties a knot in a birch-twig."[24]

4. MISCELLANEOUS CURES

In the Punjab a cure for hemorrhoids is to tie a cotton thread of five colors round the big toe at night, and to wear it for a fortnight, ending on a Tuesday.[25] A cure for a snake bite among the Veddas in Ceylon is to utter a charm and tie a string made of human hair round the limb above the bite.[26] Medicine men in Togoland carry black and white cords, and they wind magic cords round the arms of sick people so that the evil spirits will depart from their bodies.[27] In the Highlands of Scotland black and white thread used to be wound round the limbs of people and animals who were thought to have been touched by the evil eye.[28] The Musquakie Indians wore magic headbands to cure headaches.[29] The *izze-kloth*, or sacred medicine cord of the Apaches, was believed capable of working all kinds of miracles, including the healing of the sick.[30] The *'ukād* in modern Egypt is a woolen cord with seven knots, over each of which a charm has been uttered, and each of which has been blown on by a magician. It is used to cure colds and fevers, and is often hung round the necks of children.[31]

An ancient Assyrian cure for ophthalmia was to twist black and white hairs together, tie "seven and seven" knots in them while uttering a charm, and fasten the black hair to the sick eye and the white hair to the sound eye.[32] To cure an unspecified ailment, a Babylonian priest spoke the words "Ea hath sent me" three times, and untied a knot that had previously been tied. Then the sick man had to go away without looking back.[33]

The elder Pliny (died 79 A. D.), in his extensive account of ancient folk medicine, includes several magic remedies that involve knots.[34] For catarrh and ophthalmia, he says, the "magicians" recommend that the fingers of the right hand be tied together with a linen thread. For sores on the thighs due to riding a horse, they say that the groin should be rubbed with the foam from a horse's mouth, and three horsehairs, in which three knots are tied, should be placed in the sore. For quartan fever, wrap a caterpillar in linen, pass a thread three times round it, and tie three knots, repeating each time the reason for doing so. Or wrap a nail or cord from a crucifixion in wool, tie it round the patient's neck, and after the patient is cured, hide it in a hole where the sun cannot shine on it. For inguinal tumors, take a thread from a loom, tie seven or nine knots in it, at each knot naming a widow, and attach it to the groin. For swellings of the groin, tie the big toe and the toe next to it together. To facilitate the capture of a hyena, a hunter should tie seven knots in his girdle and seven knots in his whip.

Magic remedies, Pliny admits in a moment of candor, are usually fraudulent. "And by Heavens!" he says, "the disappointment is well deserved if they prove to be of no avail." Such skepticism is commendable, in the first century A. D., of course; but unfortunately the innocent were as likely as the gullible to suffer the consequences of the quackery of the "magicians" (as Pliny called the medicine men of antiquity). Thus the mummy of a little girl who died about 1000 B. C. was found some years ago by the Egyptian Expedition of the Metropolitan Museum of Art.[35] Knotted strings were tied round her throat, elbows, wrists, and ankles, and each string had a magic number of knots in it—seven, fourteen, twenty-one—in the empty hope, presumably, of binding the sickness demon and rendering it harmless. But if the knots did the child no good, at least they did her no harm—no harm, that is, in comparison with the harm her physician did her if he prescribed, as he probably did, any of the nostrums that Pliny says were made in ancient times of sputum, blood, urine, and other equally loathsome ingredients.

During an epidemic of smallpox in Malaya in 1899, to cite a modern example, many small children who had contracted the disease were set adrift in boats in order that they might take the disease away with them. Sheltering them if they drifted back to shore was a crime punishable by death. "Slip-knots tied in strips of cocoanut leaf" were placed in the boats, "some of them having been ceremonially pulled undone in contact with the patient's forehead to loose the disease from him, and some of them still untied [i.e., tied?], probably to keep the spirit fast in the ship."[36]

5. KNOT AMULETS

Knots, so primitive people have always believed, possess preventive as well as curative powers. They have been widely used, therefore, as amulets, for protection against illness, hostile spirits, the evil eye, the spells of witches, and other malign influences. The knots discussed in the preceding sections are intended by those who tie them to cure ills already incurred. Apotropaic knots, as amuletic knots are sometimes called, are tied as a precaution against present and future dangers.

The relationship between knots and amulets is an intimate one. Linguistic evidence suggests that knots were among the earliest and most important prehistoric amulets. In Russia the words for amulet (*náuzŭ*) and knot (*úzelŭ*) are etymologically related, and one of the words for wizard is *Uzol'nik* (knot-tier).[37] In Hebrew literature the charmer or enchanter is called *hober haber*, "which means a man who ties (magic) knots."[38]

The prophet Isaiah (47:19) denounces Babylon for the multitude of its sorceries and the great abundance of its enchantments, but according to Gandz, the passage means, translated literally, "the great abundance of its knots."[39] "In postbiblical Aramaic literature," says Gandz, "the amulet is called *qami'a*, meaning originally a knot and then something suspended or attached by a knot."[40] In present-day Indonesia, all magic charms are called "knot-tying."[41]

Among some thirty or more Egyptian hieroglyphics which represent string, cord, rope, and the like, at least five have amuletic significance.[42] The sign ⧖, which represents either a rope hobble for cattle or just a string of magic knots, means "amulet" or "protection." The *ankh* sign ☥, which represents some sort of tie or strap, means "life, living." Egyptian artists often picture it in the hands of men, women, and deities, and the life of every individual, human or divine, was thought to depend on the possession of it. A variant of the *ankh* sign, known as the *tyet* amulet 𓎟 , signifies "life" and "welfare." Both the *ankh* sign and the *tyet* amulet are found in art as early as the Third Dynasty.

The sign 𓏤 represents a ribbon or piece of folded cloth or cord, and like the *ankh* sign is often depicted in the hands of gods and men. It, too, has amuletic significance, for it is used in the abbreviated cliché ☥𓊽𓏤, which stands for "may he live, be prosperous, be healthy." The names of Egyptian kings, furthermore, were inscribed in round or oblong spaces called *cartouches*, encircled by a double rope, which served, it has been suggested, as a magical protection for the king's name.

The Greek word δεσμός means, literally, "knot," but also "spell" or "charm," and κατάδεσις means both "binding fast" and "enchantment." The word ἅμμα means merely "knot," but the compound περίαμμα means "something worn about the body" or "amulet." And ἱμάς, which means "strap" or "thong," is also the word for Aphrodite's magic girdle.

The Latin words *fascia* and *fascina* mean "band" or "bandage" and "bundle of sticks" respectively. *Fascino* means "bewitch," *fascinatoi* means "enchanter," and *fascinum* means "witchcraft." The etymological kinship of *fascino* to *fascia* and *fascina* is dubious, but the Romans probably did not think so. In English, the original meaning of "fascinate" was "bewitch." The skeptical Lucretius, in the first century B. C., refers obliquely to magic knots as follows: *Artis religionum animum nodis exsolvere pergo* (I hasten to free the mind from the tight knots of religion).[43]

Several ancient Egyptian amulets made of knotted strings have been found and are preserved in European museums. One of them, in Berlin, has seven overhand knots and a square knot joining the ends,[44] very similar, presumably, to the modern 'uḳād mentioned on page 49 above. Several others, which are in the Egyptian collection at University College, London, are pictured in Petrie's book *Amulets*.[45]

6. THE HERCULES KNOT

In addition to these string amulets, some remarkable square knots and square-knot forms made of gold and wood have been found in Egypt from time to time. Howard Carter, for example, found two flat gold "amuletic knots of unknown meaning" on Tut-Ankh-Amen's mummy, on either side of the thorax, parallel to the arms.[46] A line drawing of one of them, showing the square-knot motif in the center, is included among the illustrations of the Hercules knot on page 57 below (Fig. 2).

Seventeen small square knots from the Twelfth Dynasty (about 2000 B. C.) were found by Morgan at Dahshur.[47] They are of hollow gold, about three centimeters long, and were formerly thought to have belonged to a necklace. Fifteen of them represent the square knot alone, with the ends cut off short. One represents the stems of two lotus blossoms knotted together, and one represents the stems of two papyrus blossoms knotted together. Similar gold knots have subsequently been found at other sites, and different conjectures have been offered as to their purpose. Winlock, commenting on several from El Lāhūn, believes that they may have been used as catches on garments, or as shoulder clasps for light dresses.[48] But whatever their practical function may have been, there can be no doubt that they had amuletic significance. Two of them are pictured on page 57 below (Fig. 4).

Three square knots made of wood, about 14.5 centimeters long, were found at Deir el Bahri by the Egyptian Expedition of the Metropolitan Museum of Art. They are inscribed with the name of Queen Hat-shepsūt, and date from about 1500 B. C. A line drawing of one of them is provided on page 57 (Fig. 3).

The Greeks and Romans called the square knot the Hercules knot (Greek Ἡρακλεωτικόν ἅμμα or Ἡράκλειος δεσμός; Latin *nodus Herculis, Herculeus,* or *Herculaneus*) and thought that it had beneficent magic power. Pliny, in his *Natural History,* says that wounds are supposed to heal with remarkable rapidity if they are bound with a Hercules knot, and that it is useful to tie the girdle with it every day, "for," he adds, "Demetrius wrote a treatise in which he states that the number four is one of the prerogatives of Hercules."[49] Demetrius is believed to have been a physician who lived about 200 B. C., but the relevance of the number four to the square knot is obscure. The point may be, perhaps, that the square knot is, in fact, square: it has four corners from which four cords project, one from each corner.

The ancients may have attributed special amuletic power to the Hercules knot because Hercules, its supposed inventor, was worshiped as a savior (σωτήρ) and averter of evil (ἀλεξίκακος). Or they may have thought that, like the cowrie shell, it resembled the female generative organs. A Roman bride customarily wore a girdle of wool tied with a Hercules knot, and upon arriving at her husband's house, she anointed the doorposts and tied woolen threads round them. In the bridal chamber her husband untied the Hercules knot in her girdle as an omen of fruitfulness.[50]

The square knot is the only knot that is realistically portrayed in ancient art. In Egypt it is shown as a shoulder knot, a girdle knot, a necklace knot, and independently (as we have seen) as a golden or wooden amulet. It is often used as part of the design of Egyptian thrones, and it symbolizes, when so used, the union of Lower and Upper Egypt. It is worked into the handles of a number of vases of a kind called, appropriately, the Hercules vase (σκύφος Ἡρακλεωτικός); it sometimes joins the heads of the two serpents in Mercury's caduceus or wand; it is the girdle knot in many statues of deities and mortals (Athena and Roman vestals, for example); and it turns up in rings, clasps, bracelets, and other kinds of jewelry. Drawings illustrative of these uses will be found on pages 55-57.

Greek and Roman artists had little occasion to depict any knots other than the Hercules knot. Egyptian artists did, and yet they deliberately refrained from doing so. When they represented a knot in an otherwise realistic scene of daily life on the wall of a mastaba or tomb, they avoided realism and resorted to meaningless and conventionalized curves. "As the Egyptian artists, in both the Old and Middle Kingdom, were accurate in detail," writes Margaret Murray, "we can only suppose that these subterfuges were intentional, and were due not to incapacity on the part of the artist to represent so small an object but to some religious or superstitious feeling in representing a knot that could never be untied."[51] This taboo, however, if that is what it was, evidently did not apply to the square knot. (Examples of the way Egyptian artists avoided realism when drawing knots are shown on pages 58-59.)

THE HERCULES KNOT

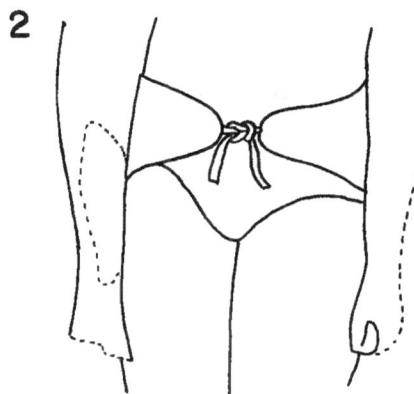

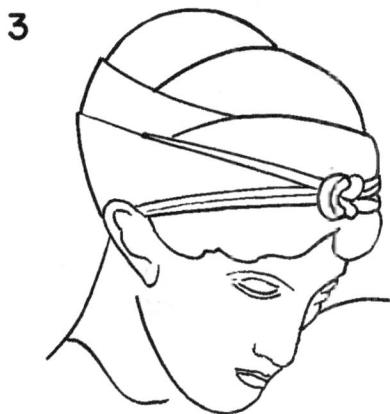

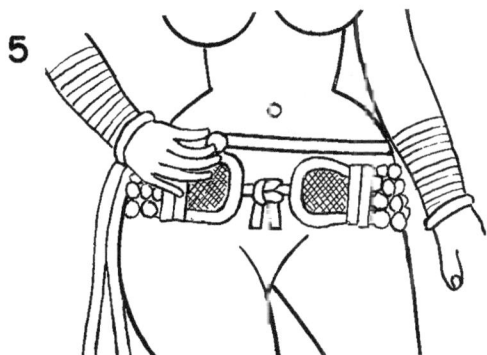

1

2

3

4

5

6

THE HERCULES KNOT

1

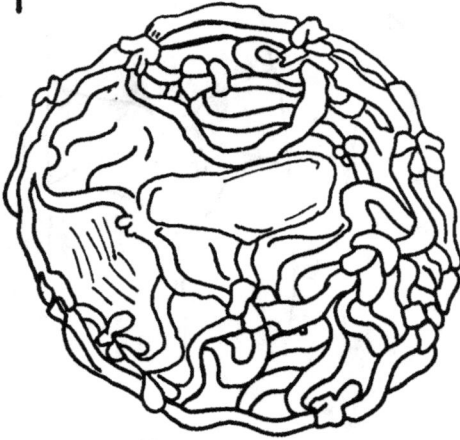
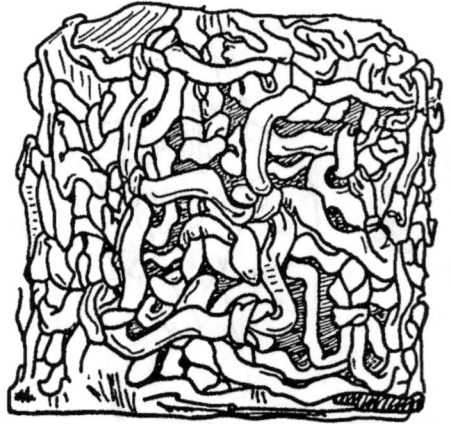

2   3   4

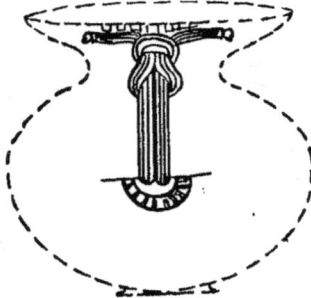

5

THE HERCULES KNOT

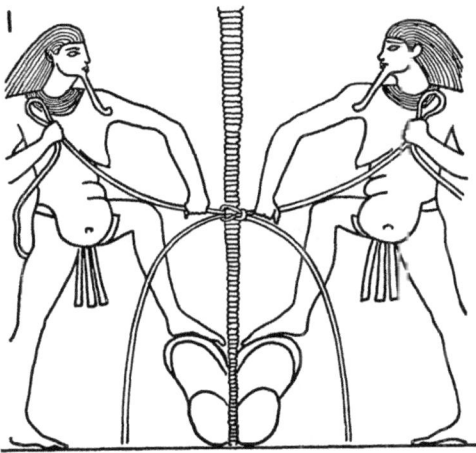

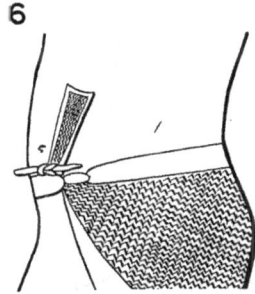

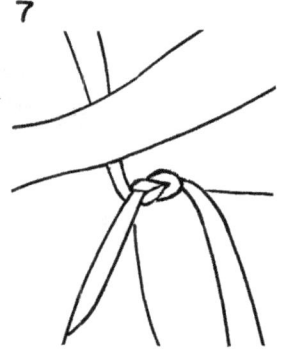

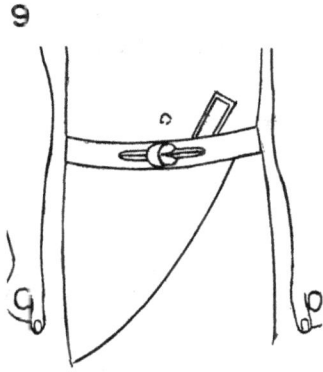

CONVENTIONALIZED KNOTS

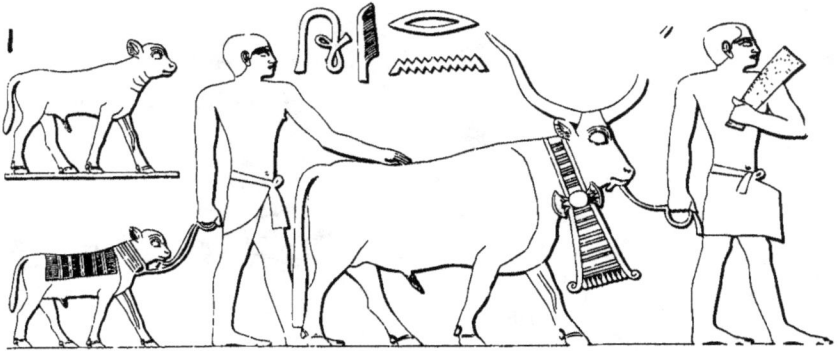

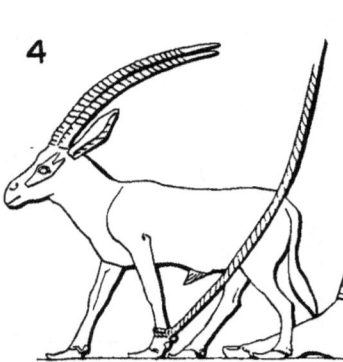

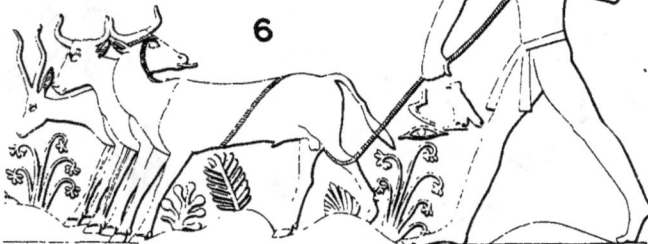

CONVENTIONALIZED KNOTS

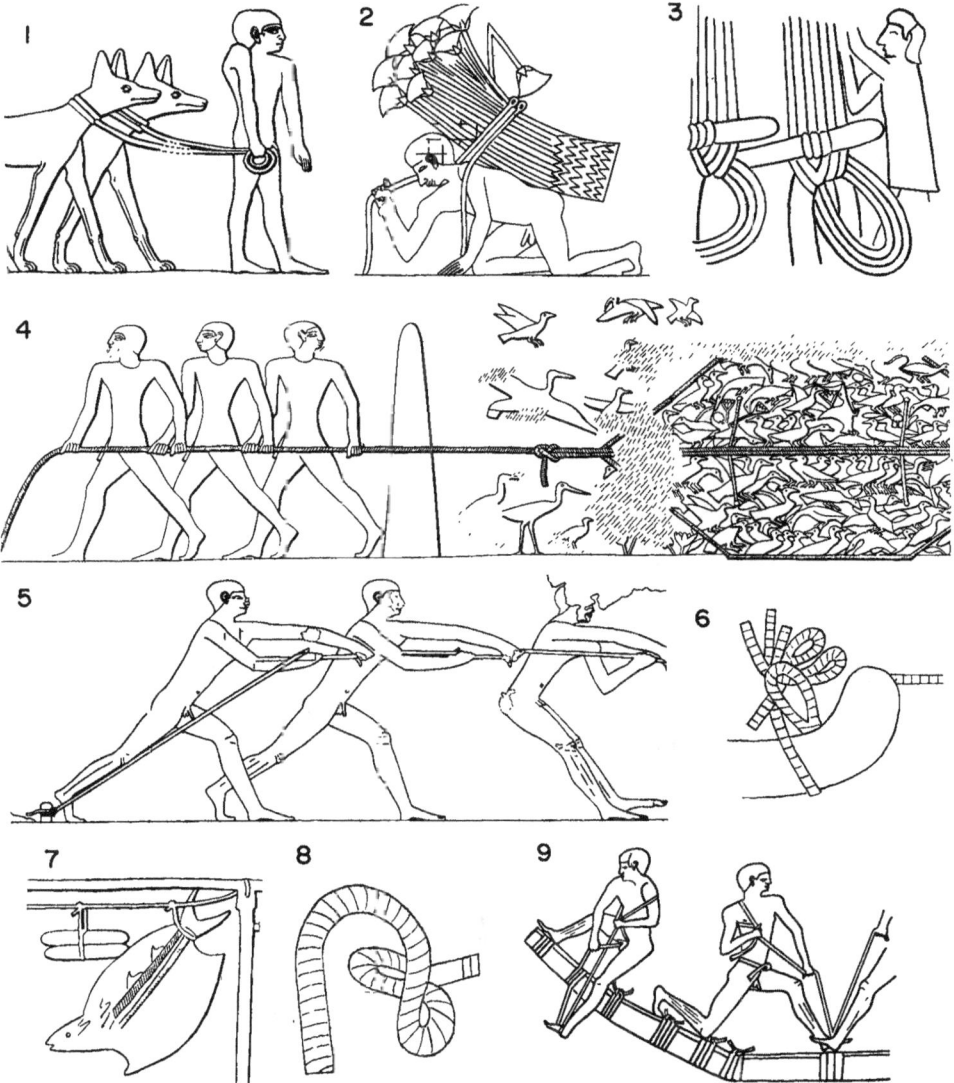

SACRAL KNOTS

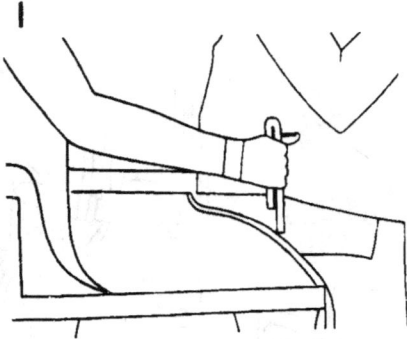

THE HERCULES KNOT
(see page 55)

1. A colossal statue of Herakles from Cyprus, with damaged nose and mouth, wearing a lion's skin. About 600 B. C. The paws are tied together with a Hercules knot *(Herakleios desmos, Herakleotikon hamma, nodus Herculeus, nodus Herculaneus).* The Metropolitan Museum of Art, the Cesnola Collection; purchased by subscription, 1874-1876.
2. The torso of a youthful votary, lacking head and feet, found at Old Paphos in Cyprus by J. H. Iliffe and T. B. Mitford, leaders of the Kouklia Expedition (1950). The "Cypriote belt" or loin cloth is tied with a Hercules knot. About 600 B. C. From a photograph in *The Illustrated London News,* January 20, 1951, p. 105. The Metropolitan Museum of Art owns an earlier statue of a Cypriote votary (about 750 to 700 B. C.) with loin cloth and Hercules knot.
3. The head of a Greek bride, 5th century B. C., now in the Olympia Museum. The Hercules knot was associated with virginity in Greece and Rome. From a photograph in Gerhart Rodenwaldt, *Die Kunst der Antike (Hellas und Rom),* Propyläen Verlag, Berlin, 1927, p. 272.
4. The virgin goddess Athena. A Roman copy of Myron's statue in the group "Athena and Marsyas." From a photograph in Gerhart Rodenwaldt, *Die Kunst der Antike (Hellas und Rom),* Propyläen Verlag, Berlin, 1927, p. 306. The Hercules knot has the form of a bowknot in a Roman copy of a Greek statue of Athena in the Metropolitan Museum of Art.
5. The statue of a goddess, now in Lucknow, from a Buddhist temple in the north of India near Mathura. Date: 3rd century A. D. From a photograph in *Réalités,* July, 1965, p. 56.
6. The girdle of a vestal virgin (Rome). From a drawing in Hjalmar Öhrvall, *Om Knutar,* 1916, p. 204. Öhrvall cites Heinrich Jordan, *Der Tempel der Vesta und das Haus der Vestalinnen,* 1886, Figs. 2, 7, 9, 10, and 17, which, he says, illustrate statues of vestals with knotted girdles.

THE HERCULES KNOT
(see page 56)

1. Top and side views of a marble representation of the sacred Omphalos (or navel of the earth). Knots that have the approximate form of Hercules knots may be seen here and there in the netlike fillet that is carved in relief on the surface of the stone. From a sketch in Otto Benndorf and Richard Schöne, *Die Antiken Bildwerke des Lateranensischen Museums,* 1867, Plate 11. The Omphalos was associated with the cult of Apollo in

fifth-century Greece. A representation of it (now lost) stood between two golden eagles near the sacrificial hearth and the golden statue of Apollo in the temple of Apollo at Delphi. Another representation, which Pausanias saw outside the temple in the second century (*Description of Greece*, X.xvi.3), has been found and is now in the Museum at Delphi. Euripides, Strabo, Plutarch, and other ancient authors mention the Omphalos; nearly every Greek city had a copy of it; and it is depicted (with many variations) on coins, vases, and reliefs—covered, as a rule, by a fillet of wool, which (like the Hercules knot) was thought to possess special protective and curative powers. See Daremberg and Saglio's *Dictionnaire des Antiquités Grecques et Romaines, s. v.* "Omphalos," IV (n. d.), pp. 197-200.

2. Mercury's caduceus or wand. A Hercules knot, in this representation, joins the heads of the two serpents. From a sketch in Daremberg and Saglio's *Dictionnaire des Antiquités Grecques et Romaines, s. v.* "nodus," IV, Fig. 5323. According to Athenagoras's *Apology* (XX), the knot in the caduceus symbolizes the union of Jupiter and Rhea, for Jupiter bound Rhea to himself with a Hercules knot. Macrobius, on the other hand (*Convivia Saturnalia*, I.xix.16), says that the caduceus represents the union of the male and female serpent and symbolizes necessity.

3. The handle of an ancient vase in the Naples Museum. From a sketch in Daremberg and Saglio's *Dictionnaire des Antiquités Grecques et Romaines, s. v.* "nodus," IV, Fig. 5324. Athenaeus (XI.500a) calls vases of this sort *skyphoi Herakleotikoi* (σκύφοι Ἡρακλεωτικοί).

4. A clasp with Hercules knot and Gorgon's head. From a sketch in Darembeg and Saglio's *Dictionnaire des Antiquités Grecques et Romaines, s. v.* "nodus," IV, Fig. 5327. Both the Gorgon's head and the Hercules knot were believed to possess amuletic power against the evil eye. The British Museum owns more than thirty Phoenician, Greek, Etruscan, and Roman earrings, bracelets, clasps, necklaces, rings, and sandal ornaments which employ the motif of the Hercules knot. See F. H. Marshall, *Catalogue of the Jewelry ... in ... the British Museum*, 1911.

5. A silver bowl, with Hercules knot design, in the Hildesheim collection in Berlin. From a photograph in Gerhart Rodenwaldt, *Die Kunst der Antike (Hellas und Rom)*, Propyläen Verlag, Berlin, 1927, p. 573.

THE HERCULES KNOT
(see page 57)

1. Two deities tying the square knot that symbolized the union of Upper and Lower Egypt (throne of a statute of Sesostris I, 1980-1935 B. C.). From a photograph in Schäfer and Andrae, *Die Kunst des Altens Orients*, Propyläen Verlag, Berlin, 1927, p. 297. This symbol of union occurs re-

peatedly, with variations, in Egypt an art. See Penelope Fox, *Tutankhamen's Treasure*, 1951, Plate 6; Christiane Desroches-Noblecourt, *Tutankhamen*, 1963, Plates 4a, 10, 11c, and 12; and Lange and Hirmer, *Egypt*, 1961, Plates 36, 85, 86, 97, 104, 152, 190, 218, and 222.

2. One of two gold amuletic knots found beside Tutankhamen's thorax parallel to the arms. The knot depicted is a conventionalized square knot. From Howard Carter, *The Tomb of Tut-Ankh-Amen*, Cooper Square Publishers, Inc., II (1963), Plate 83a.

3. A square knot in cedar about 14 centimeters long, discovered in a foundation deposit, temple of Hat-shepsūt, Deir el Bahri, about 1500 B. C. The Metropolitan Museum of Art, Museum Excavations, 1920-1922, Rogers Fund. Two square knots in ebony, inscribed with Hat-shepsūt's name, were found by the Metropolitan's Egyptian Expedition in 1926-1927. (Accessions 22.3.258, 27.3.399.)

4. Two of several small gold knots found by Morgan in the last century, used as clasps or in necklaces, and presumably of amuletic significance. They have the square-knot form. Examples of various sizes, and different in detail, have been found by later expeditions. See J. J. M. de Morgan, *Fouilles à Dahchour*, I (1895), Plates 15 and 16; H. E. Winlock, *The Treasures of El Lāhūn*, 1934, Plates 9 and 13; and J. H. Breasted, *Geschichte Aegyptiers*, translated by Ranke, 1936, Fig. 329.

5. A wooden figure of Methethy, overseer of the estate of Unis, last king of the Fifth Dynasty. The neckpiece is fastened by a realistically represented square knot. Nelson Gallery-Atkins Museum (Nelson Fund), Kansas City, Missouri.

6. Square-knot belt fastening. From Margaret A. Murray, *Saqqara Mastabas*, II (1937), Plate 1.

7. Square-knot waist fastening. Tomb of Ramose, Thebes, Eighteenth Dynasty. From Lange and Hirmer, *Egypt*, Hirmer Verlag, Munich, 3rd edition, 1961, Plate 174.

8. Square-knot shoulder fastening. Tomb of Ptahhotep, Saqqara, Fifth Dynasty. From Lange and Hirmer, *ibid.*, Plate 72.

9. Conventionalized square-knot fastening. Statue of Ranufer, Fifth Dynasty. From Lange and Hirmer, *ibid.*, Plate 61.

10. Conventionalized square-knot shoulder fastening, Fifth Dynasty. From W. and B. Forman, *Egyptian Art*, Paul Hamlyn, Ltd., London, 1962, Plate 17.

CONVENTIONALIZED KNOTS
(see page 58)

The square knot or reef knot, as it is called in English, was sometimes accurately and realistically portrayed in Egyptian art. Other kinds of knots, ordinarily, were not. The illustrations on pages 58-59, above, tend to support Margaret Murray's thesis (see above, page 54) that Egyptian artists habitually conventionalized their representations of knots, or resorted to subterfuges, in order to avoid depicting knots that could never be untied.

1. From N. de G. Davies, *The Mastabas of Ptahhetep and Akkathetep at Saqqareh,* Egypt Exploration Society, II (1901), Plate 21.
2. From M. A. Murray, *Saqqara Mastabas,* British School of Archaeology in Egypt and B. Quaritch, II (1937), Plate 4.
3. From *ibid.,* Plate 5.
4. From *ibid.,* Plate 5.
5. From N. de G. Davies, *The Mastabas of Ptahhetep and Akkathetep at Saqqareh,* Egypt Exploration Society, I (1900), Plate 22.
6. From *ibid.,* Plate 22.
7. From A. M. Blackman, *The Rock Tombs of Meir,* Egypt Exploration Society, II (1915), Plate 3.

CONVENTIONALIZED KNOTS
(see page 59)

1. From M. A. Murray, *Saqqara Mastabas,* British School of Archaeology in Egypt and B. Quaritch, II (1937), Plate 4.
2. From A. M. Blackman, *The Rock Tombs of Meir,* Egypt Exploration Society, II (1915), Plate 3.
3. From Edouard Naville and H. R. Hall, *The XIth Dynasty Temple of Deir El-Bahari,* Egypt Exploration Society, III (1913), Plate 13.
4. From M. G. Maspéro, *Le Musée Égyptien Recueil de Monuments et de Notices sur les Fouilles d'Égypte,* III (1915), Plate 36. Volume I of this bibliographically confusing work was published by Eugène Grébaut in 1890-1900, and Volume II by Pierre Lacau in 1907. The knot shown here is known in English by various names: sheet bend, weaver's knot, becket hitch, simple bend, common bend, swab hitch, signal-halyard bend, and perhaps others. It is the only knot other than the square knot that is realistically represented in any of the books on Egyptian art that I have consulted. Is it possible that Maspéro's draftsman could have allowed his imagination to take control of his pencil? The men depicted are hauling on a bird trap. In a similar scene from Meir, accurate representation of what must have been the same knot is carefully avoided (A. M. Blackman, *The Rock Tombs of Meir,* II, 1915, Plate 4).
5. From A. M. Blackman, *The Rock Tombs of Meir,* Egypt Exploration Society, II (1915), Plate 3.

6. From P. E. Newberry, *El Bersheh,* Egypt Exploration Society, I (1893), Plate 15.
7. From M. A. Murray, *Saqqara Mastabas,* British School of Archaeology in Egypt and B. Quaritch, II (1937), Plate 4.
8. From *ibid.,* I (1905), Plate 40.
9. From A. M. Blackman, *The Rock Tombs of Meir,* II (1915), Plate 4.

SACRAL KNOTS

(see page 60)

1. A folded cloth or cord is seen in the hands of many Egyptian statues. It was used as a hieroglyph signifying health, and may be profitably compared with the cords, whether knotted or unknotted, which in other parts of the world have been thought to possess magic power. From A. M. Blackman, *The Rock Tombs of Meir,* Egypt Exploration Society, II (1915), Plate III.
2. The Isis knot, an unidentified knot of religious or magic significance. The mantle of the Egyptian goddess Isis is customarily tied with it in Roman statues of the goddess. From Daremberg and Saglio, *Dictionnaire des Antiquités Grecques et Romaines,* III, part i (n. d.), 579, Fig. 4095, *s. v.* "Isis."
3. One of Tehuti-hotep's daughters, wearing a head-dress that looks as if it were tied with a bowknot. From P. E. Newberry, *El Bersheh,* Egypt Exploration Society, I (1893), frontispiece. Actually, according to Margaret Murray, the fastening is not a bowknot, but rather "the conventional representation of a knot." See her article "Knots" in *Ancient Egypt,* I (1922), 17.
4. The Cretan votary shown here is known to scholars as the *petite Parisienne* because of her large eye and provocative lips. She is wearing what is thought to be the mysterious sacral knot of Crete. From Arthur Evans, *The Palace of Minos,* The Macmillan Company, I (1921), Fig. 311.
5. The sacral knot of Crete as painted on the wall of the palace at Niru Khane. From Arthur Evans, *The Palace of Minos,* The Macmillan Company, II, part i (1928), Fig. 168.
6. The sacral knot, carved in ivory, from Knossos. From Arthur Evans, *The Palace of Minos,* I (1921), Fig. 308.
7. One of several faïence knots found by Schliemann at Mycenae. From Henry Schliemann, *Mycenae,* New York, 1878, p. 242. Schliemann thought they were made of alabaster. M. P. Nilsson has suggested that they were prizes for the winners of competitions (*The Minoan-Mycenaean Religion,* 1927, p. 137), but in view of the prevailing attitude toward knots in the ancient world, it is more likely that they had religious or magic significance.

65

7. THE SLIP KNOT

The mysterious Minoan knot-tassels found by Schliemann at Mycenae and by Evans in Crete are unlike anything else in ancient art.
When first found in the graves of the Acropolis at Mycenae, they were
thought to be mere ornaments.[52] Later, however, many representations
of them were found in the Palace of Minos at Knossos, some of them
embossed on gold signet rings, some of them in wall paintings, and
some of them executed in faïence and ivory.[53] Another explanation of
them, therefore, had to be found, and it is now agreed that they had
ritual or magic significance. Nilsson's suggestion that they were either
prizes or a detail of contemporary fashion does not accord with the
attitude toward knots of other ancient people.[54]

When viewed in perspective against the background of magic knots
in general, the knotted tassels of Mycenae and Knossos are seen to be
remarkable in an important respect: they are loop knots. They consist,
that is to say, of a loop, a knot, and two ends. Although their identity
cannot be established with anything like certainty, they may very well
be ordinary slip knots. If so, a pull on the shorter end would loosen
them at once.

The slip knot is never specifically mentioned by ancient authors as
possessing magic power. It is a magic knot among the Lapps, however,
and the Lapps are as likely as any modern people to have preserved the
ancient superstitions concerning knots. "A Lapp whom I questioned
concerning the knots used by Lapps," writes Öhrvall, "made a slip knot
of this sort [i.e., like the overhand slip knot that Öhrvall has just de-
scribed] . . . and said that it was called a *turknut* or *lyckoknut* [luck
knot]; also that to wear a cord tied round the neck with nine *turknutar*
tied in it was thought by many Lapps to bring luck."[55]

Öhrvall suggests that the slip knot is especially suitable as a *trollknut*
(troll knot or magic knot) because it vanishes with a pull on the end.
Knots in general are closed, and therefore dangerous; but the overhand
slip knot is the least closed and permanent of all knots. When the loop
is reduced to the smallest possible circumference (Öhrvall says that it
was so reduced in the *turknutar* tied by his informant), the slightest pull
on the end will release it. Although closure is dangerous, the closure
of a slip knot can be terminated at a moment's notice.

The Malay medicine man, says Skeat, in order to cast out the devil of sickness, makes little dough images and places them in a tray with a silver dollar and a taper. One end of a parti-colored thread is held by the patient, and the other end is placed between the taper and the dollar. The medicine man then utters magic spells to make the evil spirit pass along the thread into the objects on the tray. When he thinks this has been accomplished, he unties three slip knots, repeats another charm, and throws the remaining knots out of the house.[56]

Wolters describes a Greek vase on which a number of nude men and women are depicted with threads or strings tied round various parts of their bodies. Some of the strings have just one knot in them, others have several knots; and all, Wolters argues, represent amulets.[57] Identification of the knots on the basis of Wolters' illustrations is impossible, but since some of them consist of a loop, a knot, and two ends, they may be slip knots. If so, they provide an interesting analogy to the ritual knots of Mycenae and Knossos.

8. Miscellaneous Amulets

Colored cords (whether knotted or unknotted) and nets (because of their many knots) have always been esteemed as amulets. White cords customarily symbolize health, black cords disease and death, and red cords the blood of life. Cords made of wool are thought to possess especially great magic power. The following Assyrian charm shows that these conventions had become fixed at a very early date:

> Bind white wool doubled in spinning on his bed, front and sides,
> Bind black wool doubled in spinning on him,
> On his left hand,
> That there may enter no evil spirit, nor evil demon,
> Nor evil ghost, nor evil devil, nor evil god, nor evil fiend,
> Nor hag-demon, nor ghoul, nor robber-sprite,
> Nor incubus, nor succuba, nor phantom-maid,
> Nor sorcery, nor witchcraft, nor magic, nor calamity,
> Nor spells that are not good—
> That they may not lay their head to his,
> Their hand to his,
> Their feet to his,
> That they may not draw nigh.[58]

In modern times, black woolen cords with knots in them have been used as amulets in the Hebrides,[59] and red and red-and-white cords, with knots, in Macedonia.[60] Cotton cords, half yellow and half white, and knotted at intervals, are worn by pregnant women in Togoland to protect themselves and their unborn children from evil influences.[61] Musquakie Indians wore leg and head bands of special patterns and colors, and when asked why they did so, they always replied: "Luck band, luck band, bring heap good luck."[62]

Bridal couples and pregnant women require special protection against magic spells, and nets as well as knots have often been used to keep evil influences away from them. In parts of Russia, for example, a fish net used to be thrown over a bride after she was dressed because, presumably, all the knots in the net would have to be untied before she could be harmed. The groom and his companions were also provided with nets.[63] The modern bridal veil reflects the once universal belief in such superstitions. Brides in ancient Israel wore knotted cords,[64] and both bride and groom in aboriginal Australia wore amuletic red bands on their foreheads.[65]

In pre-Communist China, the sedan chair in which a pregnant woman was carried was sometimes enclosed in a net.[66] In northern India women hung up nets before childbirth to repel evil spirits,[67] and in Luzon women had nets tattooed on their arms for the same reason.[68]

The upper-class boy in ancient Rome wore a golden amulet called a *bulla* round his neck, but the son of poor parents had to be content with a knotted cord.[69] Jewish children in Talmudic times wore knotted cords round their necks.[70] In Togoland, cords are tied round the necks, arms, and feet of newborn babies in order to protect them from the charms of evil witches and wizards.[71]

Knots and nets were once widely used to keep harmful spirits away from houses, cattle, and crops. In Armenia, Russia, and Bulgaria magic knots were believed capable of tying shut the mouths of predatory wolves.[72] In central Africa a cord, hung on the door, was supposed to turn into a snake if a thief tried to enter in order to steal something.[73] The Tena Indians of Alaska hung small nets over the doors and windows of their houses because they thought that evil demons, if they tried to get in, would become enmeshed in the knots.[74] In Scotland, hemp cords which had been plaited with the left hand were tied round the necks of cattle at sundown in order to keep witches out of the barns.[75] The Toradjas of Indonesia tie knotted palm leaves to poles at the entrances to rice paddies, and knotted grass to the doors of barns, because they imagine that the souls of the dead, which might want to return to earth in order to ruin the crops, would remain outside for fear of being caught in the knots.[76]

To learn the proper time to sow seeds, the Toradja farmer in Indonesia goes to a priest at dusk and listens to the hoot of an owl. When he hears an auspicious hoot, he ties a knot in a blade of grass, buries the grass in the soil to be cultivated, and imagines that the success of the crop is bound up in the knot.[77] If a traveler hears an inauspicious cry of a bird, he must remain for a night where he is, in order to give the evil time to spread and become harmless. But if he has to go on, he can tie a knot in some long grass, spit on it, put a chew of *sirih-pinang* beside it, and proceed on his way. The evil will remain tied up in the knot and in the deeply rooted grass.[78]

To prevent the soul of the rice from departing and impoverishing the harvest, a Toradja girl goes alone to the paddy, binds from three to seven stalks of rice together, and ties some knots in them. In this way the soul of the rice is thought to be bound to the soil. The knotted plants remain uncut until the whole harvest has been gathered. At the end of every day's work, a knot is tied in the rice that has been cut last, and before the harvest is stored, herbs with knots in them are placed on the floor of the bin to tie the body and the soul of the rice together.[79]

Even death can be repelled, so it used to be believed, by means of knots and knotted cords. Strings with knots in them were discovered round the neck of a convicted Scottish witch in 1572, and when they were taken away from her she lost all hope of being saved from death.[80] During the Russo-Japanese War, the women of Japan prepared amuletic body-bands for their sons and husbands as a protection against cuts, thrusts, and bullets.[81] The Russian insurgent chief Stenka Razin thought that the following charm would make him invulnerable:

"I attach five knots to each hostile, infidel shooter, over arquebuses, bows, and all manner of warlike weapons. Do ye, O knots, bar the shooter from every road and way, lock fast every arquebuse, entangle every bow, involve all warlike weapons, so that the shooters may not reach me with their arquebuses, nor may their arrows attain to me, nor their warlike weapons do me hurt. In my knots lies hid the mighty strength of snakes—from the twelve-headed snake."[82]

9. MALEFICIUM

The mysterious power that is supposed to reside in knots, either because of the *mana* in them or because a sorcerer has uttered spells and charms over them, can be injurious as well as beneficial. Inconsistencies in usage sometimes arise as a result of this dichotomy. For example, in some communities brides wore nets in order to safeguard themselves from the evil eye and the malevolence of witches, whereas in others they made a point of untying all the knots and fastenings in their clothing just before the marriage ceremony. Such inconsistencies are due at least in part to the fact that the supposed effectiveness of a magic knot depends as much on the intentions of the person who ties the knot as on the virtues inherent in the knot itself.

Occasional instances are reported of the belief that knots can cause an enemy's death. Thus in Lapland certain women who were reputed to be witches, and no doubt thought of themselves as such, tied three knots in a linen towel in the name of the devil, spat on the knots, and "called the name of him they doomed to destruction."[83] Here the infernal invocation, the act of spitting, and the uttering of the victim's name determined the effect the knots were supposed to have. The act of spitting is to be interpreted as a way of imbuing the knots with something of the witch's own spiritual essence. Frazer in *The Golden Bough* calls attention to an allusion in the Koran to the mischief of "those who puff into knots." An Arab commentator on the passage, he says, explains that the words refer to women who tie magic knots and then blow and spit on them.[84]

In Togoland it was believed that a medicine man could kill an enemy by tying a knot in a stalk of grass and then pronouncing the following curse: "I have tied up So-and-So in this knot. May all evil light upon him! When he goes into the field, may a snake sting him! When he goes to the chase, may a ravening beast attack him! And when he steps into the river, may the water sweep him away! When it rains, may the lightning strike him! May evil nights be his!"[85]

In parts of Germany, as late as the nineteenth century, it was believed that an enemy could be killed by means of a knot in the branch of a willow tree.[86] And in India, Persia, Arabia, Africa, Australia, New Guinea, and elsewhere, magic nets, snares, and knots have been, and in some instances probably still are, used as lethal weapons.[87]

As a rule, however, witches and wizards have tied maleficent knots, not in order to kill people, but in order to inhibit their sex life, and in particular to render bridegrooms impotent. This kind of magic was called *Nestelknüpfen* in Germany during the Middle Ages, *nouer l'aguillette* in France, *nålknytning* in Sweden, and *asar* in medieval Hebrew. The legal term was *ligatura*. To make a ligature was held to be a serious crime under Salic law in the fifth century,[88] and Theodore of Tarsus pronounced the practice detestable in the seventh century.[89] It was made punishable by excommunication in 1208,[90] and by death according to a decree of the Council of Regensburg.[91]

Prosecutions for the crime are recorded as late as the seventeenth and eighteenth centuries. At the trial of Helen Isbuster on the Orkney Islands in 1635, it was charged that a man had been ruined by nine magic knots tied in a blue thread. In 1705 George and Lachlan Ratray were sentenced to death in Scotland for bewitching a man named Spalding, and destroying his wedded bliss, by means of magic knots. In 1718 the Parlement of Bordeaux sentenced a person to be burned alive for using knots to bewitch an entire family.[92]

The severity of these sentences shows how great the fear of ligatures once was. Even comparatively enlightened people, while deploring the use that was made of them, believed in their efficacy. James I of England speaks in his book on demonology of the harm done by such "Devil's rudiments" as "staying maried folkes, to have naturallie adoe with other, by knitting so manie knottes vpon a poynt at the time of their mariage."[93] Jean Bodin, on the other hand, with what seems like a measure of skeptical objectivity, refers to a peasant woman who told him in 1567 that there were more than fifty ways of tying a knot so as to affect either a husband or a wife, and that the spell could be made to last for a day, a year, or forever.[94]

I detect a note of skepticism also in a story told by Snorri Sturleson (1179-1241) about the brother kings of Norway, Sigurd and Eystein, who boasted to each other of their deeds at a banquet following Sigurd's return from the First Crusade early in the twelfth century:

71

Sigurd: You must have heard that on this expedition I was in many a battle in the Saracen's land, and gained the victory in all; and you must have heard of the many valuable articles I acquired, the like of which were never seen before in this country, and I was the most respected wherever the most gallant men were; and, on the other hand, you cannot conceal that you have only a home-bred reputation.

Eystein: I have heard that you had several battles abroad, but it was more useful for the country what I was doing in the meantime at home. I built five churches from the foundations, and a harbour at Agdanes, where it before was impossible to land, and where vessels ply north and south along the coast. I set a warping post and iron ring in the sound at Sinholm, and in Bergen I built a royal hall, while you were killing bluemen for the devil in Serkland. This, I think, was of but little advantage to our kingdom.

King *Sigurd* said: On this expedition I went all the way to Jordan and swam across the river. On the edge of the river there is a bush of willows, and there I twisted a knot of willows, and said this knot thou shouldst untie, brother, or take the curse thereto attached.

King *Eystein* said: I shall not go and untie the knot which you tied for me; but if I had been inclined to tie a knot for thee, thou wouldst not have been king of Norway at thy return to this country, when with a single ship you came sailing into my fleet.

Thereupon both were silent, and there was anger on both sides.[95]

Eystein was a reasonable man, on the whole, and he probably had as little fear of ligatures as any one. Still, his anger is understandable, for there are some things that even a brother cannot be permitted to jest about.

Robert Burns's stanza in his "Address to the Deil," to which reference has already been made, runs as follows:

> Thence mystic knots mak great abuse
> On young guidmen, fond, keen, an' crouse;
> When the best wark-lume i' the house,
>   By cantrip wit,
> Is instant made no worth a louse,
>   Just at the bit.

Once a man has been bewitched by a magic knot, the proper remedy is to untie the knot and throw the cord away in some remote place. A

Babylonian incantation against witches who cast spells with magic knots ends thus: "Her knot is loosed, her sorcery is brought to nought, and all her charms fill the desert."[96] And at the trial of one Marioun Peebles in 1644, it was brought out that untying witch-knots would undo the damage wrought by them.[97]

A Jewish enchanter by the name of Lubaid bewitched the prophet Mohammed by tying eleven knots in a cord and hiding the cord in a well. Mohammed's symptoms were weakness, loss of appetite, and neglect of his wives. Fortunately the Angel Gabriel revealed the place where the knots were hidden and after they were found and brought to him, Mohammed repeated the eleven verses of Suras 113 and 114. At every verse a knot untied itself, and Mohammed recovered from his indisposition.[98]

An ounce of prevention, however, is worth a pound of cure. Hence the widespread use of amulets. Special precautions were deemed advisable at weddings, for it was then that ligatures were apt to be most dangerous. In some localities, as we have seen, bridal couples wore knots and nets to avert the spells of witches. In others they did just the opposite: they untied and loosened the knots in their clothing just before the ceremony. This custom lingered on in Perthshire, according to Frazer, until the end of the eighteenth century. In Syria, more recently, a bridegroom not only untied all the knots in his wedding garment before the ceremony, but also unbuttoned all the buttons as well.[99]

Several other aspects of sex were formerly thought to be subject to the influence of magic knots. The name "Knut," for example, was originally given to Scandinavian boys whose parents already had as many children as they wanted. The mere word "knot," it was thought, would prevent further conception.[100] Abramelin the Sage is quoted as saying that Austrian wizards in 1458 tied knots in osier or willow branches in order to put "discord among married people" and to stop the flow of milk in nursing women.[101] And Willie's mother in the medieval ballad "Willie's Ladie"[102] bewitches her daughter-in-law by tying nine magic knots in her hair in order to prevent her from bearing Willie's child. Willie, who knows something about magic himself, looses his bride's "left-foot shoe" and "the nine witch-knots That was amo that ladie's locks,"

And now he's gotten a bonny young son,
And mickle grace be him upon.

In order to make childbirth easier, whether witchcraft has been at work or not, primitive people have traditionally resorted to such homeopathic expedients as opening doors, unlocking locks, freeing caged birds, loosing the hair of the other women in the household, untying knots, unbuttoning buttons, and other acts symbolic of the freeing of the embryo from the womb. Conversely any act symbolic of constraint is taboo when a birth is imminent.

Pliny says that to sit near a pregnant woman with the fingers interlaced is to be guilty of sorcery.[103] The birth of Hercules was delayed in this manner because Ilithyia, goddess of childbirth, was bribed by Juno to sit in front of Alcmena's door with her right knee over her left, and her hands clasped.[104] If, says Pliny, the husband of a woman who is near her time will "gird her about the middle with his own girdle, and unloose the same again, saying withal this charm, *I tied the knot, and I will undo it again,* and therewith go his ways, she shall soon after . . . have more speedy deliverance."[105]

10. LOVE KNOTS

The belief that magic knots can win or retain a lover is widespread and ancient. Virgil describes the efforts of a lovesick Roman maiden to regain the love of Daphnis, her swain, by means of the conventional image of wax, the colored woolen cord, the mystic number three, the charmed knots, and the uttered spell:

> Around his waxen image first I wind
> Three woolen fillets, of three colors join'd;
> Thrice bind about his thrice-devoted head,
> Which round the sacred altar thrice is led.
> Unequal numbers please the gods.—My charms,
> Restore my lovely Daphnis to my longing arms.
> Knit with three knots the fillets; knit 'em straight;
> And say, "These knots to love I consecrate."[106]

This is a mere literary exercise, but it reflects beliefs held by the common people in Virgil's day, though presumably not by Virgil himself. In modern times the love knot has often been used as a sort of game, without serious expectation of results. In Shakespeare's *Two Gentlemen of Verona,* Julia proposes to disguise herself as a boy in order to seek out the man she loves. "Why, then," her waiting-gentlewoman tells her, "your ladyship must cut your hair." "No, girl," Julia replies,

> I'll knot it up in strings,
> With twenty odd-conceited true-love knots:
> To be fantastic may become a youth
> Of greater time than I shall show to be.[107]

John Gay's *Shepherd's Week* (1714) contains the following lines:

> As Lubberkin once slept beneath a tree,
> I twitch'd his dangling garter from his knee;
> He wist not when the hempen string I drew.
> Now mine I quickly doff of inkle blue;
> Together fast I tye the garters twain,
> And while I knit the knot repeat this strain,
> *Three times a true-love's knot I tye secure,*
> *Firm be the knot, firm may his love endure.*

"Whenever I go to lye in a strange bed," a sentimental young lady admitted in 1755, "I always tye my garter nine times round the bedpost, and knit nine knots in it, and say to myself: 'This knot I knit, this knot I tye, to see my love as he goes by.' "[108] Oliver Goldsmith in *The Vicar of Wakefield* (1766) says that the farmers of the neighborhood "kept up the Christmas carol, sent true-love knots on Valentine morning, ate pancakes on Shrovetide, showed their wit on the first of April, and religiously cracked nuts on Michaelmas eve."

A distinction is drawn in Sweden, according to Öhrvall, between the love knot *(kärleksknut),* the friendship knot *(vänskapsknut),* and the betrothal knot *(trolovningsknut).*[109] The commonest love knot, he says, is the familiar knot variously called, in English, the Englishman's knot, the fisherman's knot, the true-lover's knot, and the middleman's knot. Heraklas described the true-lover's knot very clearly in the first century A. D. and called it a single *karkhesios.* It consists of a loop and two overhand knots which can be either separated or pressed close together, the one against the other. In conformity with the symbolism implied by this characteristic of the knot, says Öhrvall, a bashful Swedish sailor a hundred years ago (were sailors bashful then?) would enclose a true-lover's knot, with the overhands separated, in a letter to his sweetheart. If she returned it with the knots close together, he would know that she still loved him.

The betrothal knot was once more common, probably, than the betrothal ring. There is reason to believe, in fact, that all rings and bracelets were originally imitations of knotted cords tied by primitive men round fingers, wrists, necks, and ankles—not for decorative purposes, but as charms and amulets.[110]

During the Middle Ages, knots were used as symbols of legal contracts in general, not merely of marriage contracts. A witness in a court of law, if he could not sign his name, would tie a knot in a strap to be attached to the document as confirmation of his testimony. Hence in legal language the word *nodator* (knot-tier) came to be a synonym of *witness*.[111]

Analogies to the betrothal knot *(trolovningsknut)* are found in many parts of Asia. In Parsi and Iranian weddings, it is said, the bride and bridegroom join hands under a curtain which separates them from each other. A piece of cloth is then wrapped around the couple and tied with a symbolic double knot. Finally twists of raw yarn are wound seven times round the couple's hands, seven times round the couple, and seven times round the knot.[112]

A Brahman bridegroom hangs a small gold ornament round the neck of his bride and ties it with three knots. Before he does so, the bride's father may withdraw his consent to the marriage, but afterward the union is indissoluble. A cord is tied round the bride's waist, and as she leaves the house a verse meaning "I loosen thee" is repeated.[113]

Ceremonial knots of this sort were probably intended, originally, as protection against the evil spells that were once thought to endanger the mutual happiness of young married people. The phrase "tying the marriage knot," therefore, was at one time no mere figure of speech, but rather the description of a custom based on the belief that magic knots can have a decisive influence on the sexual relationship of a man and a woman.

11. RELIGIOUS KNOTS

Vestiges of primitive faith in the extra-natural power of knots have survived in the rituals of contemporary religions. The Jewish phylactery knots, for example, are now regarded as symbols of divinity, but originally they probably had a more materialistic purpose. The generally accepted view is that they were amulets.[114] Another possibility is that they took the place of marks previously cut on the forehead and hands as signs of Jahweh's ownership.[115] Gandz has suggested (as we have seen) that they were mnemonic knots and served to remind the worshiper of the divine commandments.[116] Whatever their original function may have been, their retention in Hebrew law can be ascribed to the desire to give a more spiritual significance to ancient supersitions which were too deep-rooted to be eradicated.

In India, when a Brahman youth reaches the age of eight, he is invested at the rite of initiation with a cord called (in Sanskrit) the *yajnopavita* and made of three strands of cotton threads which must be spun by Brahmans. The cord is passed three times round the initiate's waist, a number of knots are tied in it, traditional formulas are uttered, and a threefold knot called the *brahmagranthi* or knot of the Creator is tied on "the north side of the navel" and "drawn to the south side of it." After marriage the cord must have six strands instead of three. All castes in India wear sacred cords with knots in them.[117]

The Parsi child also, whether boy or girl, is invested with a sacred cord. It is called the *kusti*, and is elaborately symbolic of Zoroastrian beliefs and sacred texts.[118] In pre-Communistic China, one of the Buddhist funeral rites was "the untying of knots." A bowl of rice and a seven-strand cord with twenty-four copper coins tied in it were presented to a Bonze, who then recited the virtues of Buddha in releasing souls from pain and trouble, untied the knots in succession, and put the coins one by one into his vest. The ceremony was "meant to illustrate the release from all tightness and difficulties in the next world."[119] The Grand Lama of Tibet used to tie knots of silk round the necks of his votaries.[120] In both Greek and Slavic monasteries part of the ceremony of the "investiture of the Little Habit and the Great Habit" is the bestowal of a knotted cord on monk or nun.[121]

The cord of St. Francis hung from the waist to the feet. St. Francis wore it, so it is said, in memory of the cord with which Christ was bound on the Cross, but the common people of Europe attributed curative powers to it, and thought that it could work miracles. A small fifteenth-century statue of St. Francis on exhibit at the Cloisters (a branch of the Metropolitan Museum of Art in New York) has a realistically represented cord with five-, six-, and sevenfold overhand knots in it, the longest knot at the top, the shortest at the bottom, near the end of the cord.[122] "And good Saynt Frances gyrdle, With the hamlet of a hyrdle," according to an old jingle, "Are wholsom for the pyppe."[123]

Dante in Cantos XVI and XVII of the *Inferno* speaks of a cord which he wore as a girdle on his tour of the nether world and with which he had once hoped to snare the Leopard of Incontinence. Upon reaching the great abyss between Violence and Fraud, he handed the cord, knotted and coiled, to Virgil, his guide, who threw it over the edge of the cliff. In response to this signal, the monster Geryon, personification of Fraud, rose into view and carried the travelers over the abyss. Dante, it is said, may have been a novice of the Franciscan order in his younger days, and if so, his girdle may have been the cord of St. Francis. The symbolism of the episode, however, is obscure. Perhaps the apotropaic power of the knots in the cord was intended to prevent the travelers from becoming entangled in the knots *(nodi)* and in the arabesques (symbolic of fraud) on Geryon's back, breast, and sides.

An Augustinian nun at Antwerp was miraculously cured of a grievous illness in 1657 through the wearing of a cord in honor of St. Joseph, and as a result the members of the Archconfraternity of the Cord of St. Joseph are now required to wear a cord with seven knots tied in it. St. Thomas was girded with a cord by an angel as a reward for overcoming temptation. Innocent X subsequently sanctified the Confraternity of the Cord of St. Thomas. Its members wear a cord with fifteen knots in it.[124]

The "belt of St. Guthlac" was reputed to be a sovereign remedy for a headache in the Middle Ages; and "For lampes and for bottes," said John Bale in 1562, "take me Saynt Wilfride's knottes."[125]

The distinction between magic and primitive religion is difficult to define. Was magic the precursor of religion? Or was it a corruption of religion? How does its reliance on the extra-natural differ from orthodox faith in the supernatural? Magic knots pose such questions as these in an interesting way. The Latin word *religio,* for example, seems to be etymologically related to the word *religare* (to tie or bind). Tying and binding imply knots; but who, in prehistoric times, was tied by whom, and for what purpose? It used to be assumed, says Westermarck, that the worshiper was tied by his god, or bound, as the saying is, to obey his god. Westermarck argues, on the contrary, that the god was bound by the man, and that knots were merely one of a number of devices for compelling the god to do the will of the man.[126]

In support of this view he cites a practice of the common people of Morocco, who tie rags to a saint's grave in the belief that they are binding the saint to grant their petitions. If later they get what they want, they untie the rags and release the saint. Westermarck once saw many such rags tied to a pole in a cairn dedicated to the saint Mûlai 'Abd-ŭl-Kader. "A Berber saint of mine," he writes, "invoked Lälla Răḥma Yusf, a great female saint . . . and tied his turban, saying, 'I am tying thee, Lälla Răḥma Yusf, and I am not going to open the knot until thou hast helped me.'" On another occasion a person in distress knotted the leaves in a palmetto near the grave of Lälla Răḥma Yusf, saying, "I tied thee here, O saint, and I shall not release thee unless thou releasest me from the toils in which I am at present."

The prehistoric Roman worshiper, in like manner, may have supposed that he could bind *(religare)* the gods to do his will. Vestiges of such beliefs are buried in the substrata of contemporary culture, but they are inconsistent with orthodoxy. The ritual knots of mature religions have only symbolic significance at the present time.

Chapter Three: Practical Knots

1. THE AGE OF STRING

MOST OF THE TOOLS of modern civilization, observes J. E. Lips,[1] have their roots in ancient inventions that have been handed down from generation to generation in an unbroken chain ever since the dawn of time. The Age of Iron, he points out, was made possible by the Age of Bronze, and the Age of Bronze by the Age of Stone. But still earlier, and spanning a far longer period of time—reaching back, indeed, to the very beginnings of man's evolution as man—came the Age of Wood.

Wood was one of the most abundant and usable materials available to primitive man in his attempts to win dominion over the forces of nature. Even animals use wood as a tool. Beavers build houses of it; elephants rip branches from trees in order to strike pursuing dogs; chimpanzees prod with sticks from which they have stripped the leaves; and birds make nests by weaving twigs into geometrical shapes and patterns. Primitive man, by inference, must have begun to use wood for comparable purposes some hundreds of thousands of years ago.

Wood, however, is subject to decay. Hence the tools and implements assembled in archaeological museums give a misleading impression of the probable extent of its use in prehistoric times. During the Stone Age, according to Lips, more things were made of wood than of stone: e.g., the digging stick, the club, the spear, the bow, the arrow, the boomerang, the shield, the sled, the hut, the food bowl, the animal trap, the dugout, the bark canoe, and many other devices utilized by our primitive ancestors. In a sense, the Age of Stone was merely the final phase of the Age of Wood.

Vines, reeds, grass, and bark; the skins and sinews of animals; hair, both human and animal—all of them as perishable as wood—also played an important part in the advancement of primitive man's material culture. By Neolithic times in Europe (e.g., the Lake Dwellers of Switzerland), and more recently among people living at equivalent cultural levels (e.g., the Indians of North America and the Islanders of the South Pacific), these materials were used to make nets, snares, fishlines, bowstrings, baskets, mats, moccasins, belts, and necklaces; to hold the timbers of huts and the poles of tepees together; and (among other methods) to bind the points of arrows, harpoons, and spears to their shafts, and the heads of axes, adzes, and tomahawks to their handles. The Age of Wood, in fact, could almost as fittingly be called the Age of String.

2. THE OLDEST KNOTS

String implies knots, and knots must therefore be one of man's oldest tools. Just how old, it is impossible to say, for string is perishable, and archaeological evidence, as a consequence, is lacking.[2] It is safe to assume, however, that Paleolithic man used lashings[3] in order to attach handles and shafts to implements of stone and other material; hitches[4] in order to tuck the ends of lashings under the final turns; and overhand knots[5]—the most elementary of all knots—in order to contain things and hold things together. Neolithic man, as he invented new implements and developed new skills, may be presumed to have used the granny knot,[6] the square knot,[7] the lark's head,[8] the overhand loop knot,[9] the overhand slip knot,[10] and the weaver's knot (or sheet bend).[11]

These are the familiar, general-purpose knots that people everywhere have always tied—and still tie—instinctively, without being conscious of ever having learned to tie them (though most of us nowadays, if we have been properly brought up, conscientiously tie the square knot rather than the more natural granny). They are the knots, as far as I have been able to find out, that modern Stone-Age people tie (e.g., Indians, Polynesians, and Eskimos), or *did* tie until the end of the nineteenth century. And by inference they are the knots that our prehistoric ancestors tied and depended on for survival a good many unchronicled thousands of years ago.

Ethnologists, unfortunately, seldom have anything very much to say about knots in their accounts of the material culture of modern primitive people. I gather, however, from their descriptions of primitive tools and implements, most of which involve the use of cordage, that people who lead Stone-Age lives are on the one hand enormously dependent on knots, yet, on the other, need only half a dozen elementary varieties of the sort I have listed in the two foregoing paragraphs.

Gilbert Wilson, for example, in his monograph on the use of the horse and the dog by the Hidatsa Indians,[12] describes a great many halters, bridles, snares, lariats, hobbles, saddle-pack lashings, travois-pole ties, and other devices made of thongs and vegetable-fiber cords. Wilson does not discuss knots in the text of his monograph, but if one may judge by his illustrations, the lashing, the half hitch, the overhand knot, the square knot, and the lark's head sufficed for the needs of the Hidatsas at the time he studied them.

Even when ethnologists discuss knots, they are apt to leave essential questions about them unanswered. Clark Wissler, in his monograph on the Blackfoot Indians,[31] describes a number of tepee lashings which he calls by picturesque names like Blackfoot tie, Teton tie, Assiniboine tie, and Cheyenne and Arapaho tie. Referring to the Blackfoot tie, he says that "one end of a thong about 15 feet long is passed round the crossing of the tepee poles and tied with a *simple knot*" (italics mine). He does not identify this simple knot, and his illustrative sketch depicts an ambiguous configuration that is evidently intended to represent either a square knot or a granny. The ambiguity is regrettable, since it would be interesting, ethnologically, to know which of the two knots the Blackfoot Indians actually tied; whether they were aware of the distinction between them; and (if so) whether they made a conscious effort to tie the square knot in preference to the granny.

The Polynesians, like other primitive people, were dependent on knots, and used them for mnemonic as well as for utilitarian purposes. Owing, however, to prolonged contact with the crews of whaling ships (as Ralph Linton points out in his 1923 monograph on the Marquesas Islands[14]), they had begun to use European knots before ethnologists thought of collecting information about them.

This is doubly unfortunate, because the Argonauts of the Pacific, as Malinowski calls them, were among the first and most adventurous of blue-water sailors, and it would be instructive if we could find out what knots they used, originally, and how they used them. Were they acquainted with the indispensable bowline knot (the European sailor's

FAMILIAR KNOTS

1. OVERHAND KNOT

2. OVERHAND SLIP KNOT

3. SQUARE KNOT

6. TWO HALF HITCHES

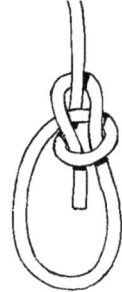

9. BOWLINE KNOT

4. GRANNY KNOT

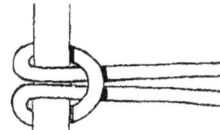

7. COW HITCH

5. WEAVER'S KNOT

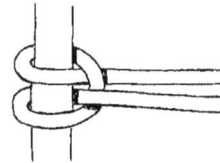

8. CLOVE HITCH

10. WALL KNOT & MATTHEW WALKER KNOT

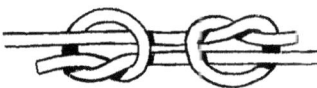

11. FISHERMAN'S KNOT

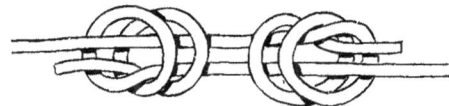

12. DOUBLE FISHERMAN'S KNOT

13. SHEEPSHANK

14. TURK'S HEAD

way of tying a fixed loop in a rope)? Did they prefer the square knot to the granny (as European sailors do)? By which of several possible techniques did they tie the weaver's knot (or sheet bend)? I have been unable to find answers to such questions as these in the published works of Linton, Buck, Handy, Malinowski, and other students of Polynesian culture.[15] I get the impression, however—though I cannot document it—that the Polynesian repertory of indigenous knots was a limited one.

The Polynesians made excellent mats, baskets, plaitings, and nets. Their string figures (or cat's cradles), in which, like other primitive people, they were fond of indulging, were numerous and intricate. If, as seems likely, they did not develop any highly specialized knots of their own, analogous to the sailors' knots of Europe and America, it must have been because they did not need them, and not because they lacked skill in the making and manipulation of cordage.

Franz Boas in 1907 published sketches of several remarkable Eskimo knots which had been collected for him in Baffin Land, and which

BOAS 1907

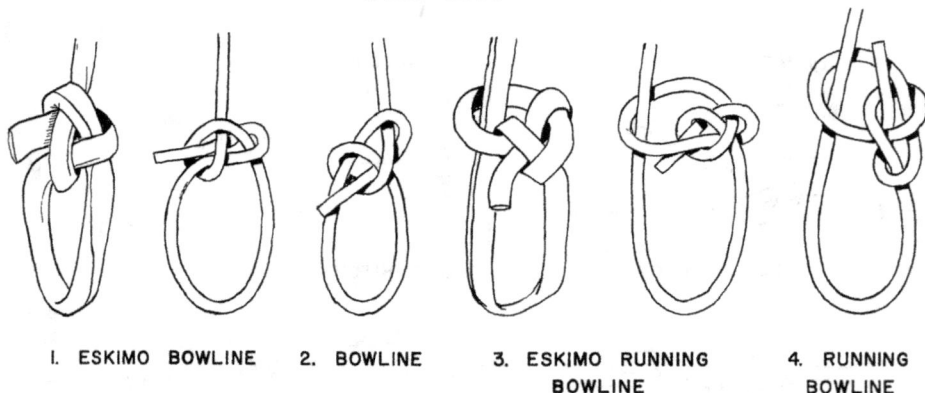

| 1. ESKIMO BOWLINE | 2. BOWLINE | 3. ESKIMO RUNNING BOWLINE | 4. RUNNING BOWLINE |

(since he himself was not versed in knot lore) Otis Mason identified for him.[16] Included were a number of rawhide "splices," a fisherman's knot, a double fisherman's knot, a square knot, and some highly unorthodox bowlines and running bowlines. I have not come upon any other references to the double fisherman's knot, the bowline, or the running bowline in any other study of the material culture of modern primitive people. These knots, therefore, possess—potentially, at least—unusual ethnological significance.

Now the Eskimo bowline and running bowline, as depicted by Boas, though identical with the European bowline and running bowline in structure, are quite different in the arrangement of their parts. That is, they are lying on their sides, as it were, in the manner shown by the diagrams on the facing page.

Unfortunately Boas does not provide the information we need in order to appraise the significance of these peculiar knots. Were they used by a single individual, or by all the members of the cultural group? Are they genuine Eskimo knots, or were they adopted as a result of imperfect imitation of the bowlines and running bowlines used by European sailors? Are they superior in any way, from the Eskimo point of view, to the European bowline and running bowline? What technique did the Eskimos use in tying them?[17] It is too late now to find the answers to such questions as these, and the same is true, I am afraid, of the questions we would like to ask concerning the knots used by other modern primitive people.[18]

3. A Physician Named Heraklas

The ancient Egyptians, Greeks, and Romans were as dependent on cordage as their Stone-Age ancestors, and a good deal more adept in the use they made of it. The Egyptians, of course, were unexcelled as weavers and rope-makers. The hulls of the earliest Egyptian river boats were held together solely by means of ropes and lashings. It was not until the Fifth Dynasty that Egyptian boat-builders began to use dowels; and boat hulls on the Red Sea were fastened by a combination of ropes and dowels as recently as five hundred years ago.[19] The great blocks of stone that went into the construction of tombs and temples, not only in Egypt but elsewhere (Stonehenge, Asia Minor, Greece, Rome, Peru), were dragged into place and erected by means of ropes.

When Xerxes invaded Greece in 492 B.C., he employed Phoenicians and Egyptians to build the pontoon bridge on which his army crossed the Hellespont. "Beginning from Abydos," writes Herodotus, "they whose business it was made bridges across to that headland, the Phoenicians one of flaxen cables, and the Egyptians the second, which was of papyrus. From Abydos to the opposite shore it is a distance of seven furlongs."[20] When a storm broke the cables and scattered the boats,

Xerxes ordered the waters of the Hellespont to be lashed with three hundred lashes, and he had the overseers beheaded.

Under new overseers, two new bridges were built, one of 360 boats and the other of 314. This time "they stretched cables from the land, twisting them taut with wooden windlasses, and they did not as before keep the two kinds apart, but assigned for each two cables of flax and four of papyrus. All these were of the same thickness and fair appearance, but the flaxen were heavier in their proportion, a cubit thereof weighing a talent." Each rope is estimated to have been a mile long and seven inches in diameter, and to have weighed as much as fifty pounds a linear foot.[21] Herodotus, unfortunately, provides no information concerning the knots used in this prodigious undertaking.

An obscure Greek physician named Heraklas, who lived during the first century A. D.,[22] is the only ancient author who has anything at all informative to say about utilitarian knots. His one extant work is a brief essay on surgeon's slings, which owes its preservation to the fact that Oribasius of Pergamum included it toward the end of the fourth century in his so-called *Medical Collections*.[23] Heraklas explains how to tie eighteen slings which Greek physicians made use of to apply traction when reducing dislocations and setting broken bones, and to hold the bodies of patients in position when performing surgical operations.

Heraklas's step-by-step instructions are reasonably lucid, and yet far from easy, without the aid of explanatory diagrams, to interpret. Two eminent men of the sixteenth century, Vidus Vidius and Francesco Primaticcio, tried to interpret them in 1540, or thereabouts, and got all but one of them wrong.

Vidius, a Florentine, was the personal physician of Francis I. He translated Oribasius into Latin, gave his name to the Vidian nerve, and became the first professor of medicine in the Collège de France. Primaticcio was the leading artist and architect resident in France during the middle years of the sixteenth century. His brilliant drawings illustrative of *Oribasius de Laqueis* ("Oribasius on Knots"), as Vidius misleadingly entitled Heraklas's essay in his translation of Oribasius, are preserved in the Bibliothèque Nationale in Paris.[24] I have reproduced them in Appendix D, below, because they possess a measure of artistic and medical significance, and because they are not available elsewhere to the general reader.

Hjalmar Öhrvall, a well-known Swedish physiologist and yachtsman, labored over Heraklas's knots in 1916, and succeeded in identifying about half of them,[25] and Lawrence Miller, a Boston patent lawyer who specialized in the patented knot-tying machines used in the textile industry, identified the remainder in 1944. Miller published only one of his identifications,[26] but he permitted me to list them in my book *The Art of Knotting and Splicing* in 1947. In Appendix D, below, I provide a detailed analysis, together with explanatory diagrams, of each identification and each knot. In the following paragraphs I shall discuss some of the more striking implications of Heraklas's essay.

From the anthropological point of view, Heraklas's most interesting knot is probably his No. 13, which he calls a "four-loop *plinthios*," and which turns out upon analysis to be a cat's cradle, or string figure—the oldest string figure, almost certainly, on record. It is identical, moreover, with a string figure from aboriginal Australia called "The Sun Clouded Over,"[27] a name that is descriptive of the way the central circle, representing the Sun in the completed figure (see my diagram in Appendix B, p. 126), gets smaller and smaller and finally disappears when the four loops at the corners are pulled apart. Heraklas, of course, was interested in the four-loop *plinthios* because he found it useful as a surgeon's sling, and not because the children of his time played, as they evidently did, the universal game of cat's cradle.

Heraklas's No. 9, the single *karkhesios*, is the traditional true-lover's knot, and he explains how to tie it by the "fancy" technique, which really isn't very fancy, known by all modern sailors. (See Appendix B, p. 118, below.) Structurally the single *karkhesios* is identical with the Eskimo fisherman's knot depicted by Boas (see p. 84), above). The two knots differ, however, in function: the former is a loop knot, the latter a knot that joins the ends of two cords. Both knots are familiar to modern anglers and fishermen.

Nos. 10-12, the double *karkhesios*, is a more esoteric knot than the single *karkhesios*. It is identical with the knot that is called (in books) the hackamore, and that is alleged to be used as a temporary rope bridle in the Western United States. It is more usually called, simply, the jug, jar, or bottle sling. Its traditional function has been to lift jugs, jars, and bottles; and that is probably what it was used for, as a rule, in ancient times, for a *karchesion* (Greek καρχήσιον; Latin *carchesium*) was a kind of vase with two long handles like the loops of a piece of string or rope.[28] Heraklas recommends it, of course, as a way of applying traction to an arm or leg, and not as a jug sling.

The double *karkhesios* is a specialized knot, unlikely to be improvised on the spur of the moment—the kind of knot that has to be deliberately learned through imitation or instruction. Heraklas speaks of it in terms that reveal his easy familiarity with it, and with knots in general. The implication is that other specialized knots were also in use at the time, and already, perhaps, had an ancient lineage. On the basis of the probabilities, we would presume that such was the case. Heraklas's double *karkhesios* provides us with explicit evidence—almost our only explicit evidence—that it was.

I say "almost" because other evidence—rather more general than specific—supports the view that the ancients were interested in esoteric knots. The Greeks, for example, played a game called *himanteligmos* in which one player tied an intricate knot and the other player tried to guess how to untie it. If he stuck a peg into the knot at the point where the secret of untying it was hidden, he was declared the winner.[29] The Gordian knot, presumably, was an intricate knot of the sort devised by the players of *himanteligmos*.

The double *karkhesios*, Heraklas says, can be tied by three different techniques: alone, from a single *karkhesios,* or round the limb itself. (See the diagrams in Appendix B, pages 119-124, below.) Professor K. G. T. Webster of Harvard showed me the first of these techniques in the early 1930's. He had learned it as a boy, he said, from an unlettered fisherman in Nova Scotia. Harry Craigin, in 1884, described how to tie it by what is essentially Heraklas's second technique.[30] Craigin's description of the knot is the first to have been published, I surmise, since Heraklas's time. The third technique does not seem to have lingered on in the folk memory. Miller's interpretation of it, as published in *The Art of Knotting and Splicing,* is unsatisfactory. A better interpretation, which I worked out only recently, is illustrated by my diagrams in Appendix B, pages 122-123, below.

Heraklas's No. 14 is the parlor magician's Tom Fool knot, and Heraklas's technique of tying it is the parlor magician's sleight-of-hand technique. Nos. 1, 2, 3, 6, and 8 are the immemorial lark's head (or cow hitch), clove hitch, overhand slip knot, overhand knot, and square knot respectively. A point of special interest is the distinction which Heraklas carefully draws between the square knot (No. 8) and the very similar nameless construction (No. 7) which consists of two interlooped bights. (See Appendix B, pages 117 and 116, for diagrams.) Modern knot-books do not always recognize this nice distinction. The ancients, however, as their faith in the magic efficacy of the square knot demonstrates, were extremely square-knot conscious.

No. 4 (the sandal sling) and No. 5 (the serpent sling) are of particular medical interest. The former is almost exactly like the bandage called Barton's cravat of the heel, and the latter is similar to the knot that is known in medical textbooks as Gerdy's extension knot. (See Appendix B, pages 113-115 below, for diagrams and additional comment.)

4 PROPRIETARY EXCLUSIVENESS

While Heraklas and Oribasius wanted to share their specialized knowledge with others, primitive and unsophisticated people are inclined to protect their specialized knowledge and to prevent outsiders from learning its secrets. The ancient Asclepiadae, or traveling physicians, were bound by oath to teach their art to Asclepiadae alone.[31] The Chinese, for many centuries, kept the secret of making silk. The Koreans discovered or stole it about 200 B. C., and the art then passed to Japan, Tibet, Persia, and Europe.[32] A method of making palm-fiber bridges in Liberia was handed down from father to son until very recently. When a bridge was being built, the people who lived near by were required to move so that they would not be able to learn how the work was done.[33] Skill in metallurgy in northern Africa was formerly the carefully guarded monopoly of specific families and clans.[34]

Proprietary exclusiveness of this sort is characteristic of sailors and others who have a specialized knowledge of knots. Ulysses, for example, tied up the gifts of Alcinous with a secret knot that Circe had taught him.[35] The Gordian knot, too, was a secret knot, for the ends of the thong were cleverly concealed and no one knew how to untie it.[36] Steinen, in his account of the Marquesas Islands, reports that a certain *tuhuka*, or "priest," considered his mnemonic knot-records superior to European writing because he alone could interpret them.[37]

A descendant of "an ancient tribe of head hunters" showed Graumont and Hensel an unusual kind of Turk's head, but agreed to explain its construction "only after our promise never to show anyone else how the weave is formed."[38] "By golly," Graumont said later to an interviewer, "those old-timers sure were jealous of anybody who wanted to learn their special knots. I'd have to show a guy a hundred different knots before he'd break down and show me one."[39]

Clifford Ashley, perhaps the last intellectual to ship out of New Bedford on an old-fashioned whaling vessel, confirms the fact that this sort of jealousy used to prevail among sailors. "Complicated knots were explained under pledge of secrecy," he says. "Often a knowledge of one knot was bartered for another. I have heard of a sailor who carried an unfinished blackjack in his ditty bag for several voyages until at last he found a shipmate who could teach him the knot he wished to finish off with."[40]

Cowboys, like sailors, are dependent on knots as a tool, and take pride in their knot-knowledge. J. M. Drew was acquainted with a cowboy who could tie the complicated Theodore knot, "and who did tie it for his brother cowboys for a good price per knot, but who would never teach anyone else how to tie it."[41]

The barrel knot, sometimes called the blood knot in England—a knot that is well known to anglers and fly fishermen—is almost the only knot that does not slip when the ends of nylon monofil leaders are tied together. Yet prior to 1910 its construction seems to have been kept a trade secret by one or two "country tackle makers" in England. "The method of construction was eventually worked out by Jock Purvis, an engineer on a White Star Liner, who cut out serial sections of the knot in paraffin wax and, after microscoping, re-built the knot in three dimensions. Purvis was an enthusiastic angler, and he told the secret of the knot to A. H. Chaytor, who published a description of the knot and how to make it, in his *Letters to a Salmon Fisher's Son,* 1910."[42]

Proprietary exclusiveness, paradoxically, tends to keep traditional skills alive and vital. Heraklas had a sophisticated modern point of view when he published, for the benefit of other physicians, what he knew about the double *karkhesios,* and other surgeon's knots. The jug sling is familiar to sailors and cowboys today, however, not because Heraklas explained it in his treatise, but because a number of unlettered individuals in every generation have known it—since long be-

90

fore Heraklas's time, presumably—and have passed their knowledge on to their descendants.

5. The End of an Era

Knots play a minor role in the daily lives of modern men and women. They are no longer used as computers and mechanical aids to the memory; the superstitions that were once associated with them have been largely forgotten; and a thousand gadgets ranging in impressiveness from waterproof glue and zippers to welding irons and pneumatic riveters have displaced them as tools for holding things together. Even sailors, nowadays, need to know only a dozen or so of the most essential knots.

Knots reached the final stage of their development during the era of the clipper ships in the second quarter of the nineteenth century. The knot-lore that was preserved in men's memories at that time has not, however, been entirely lost. Most of it is recorded in the 3,854 entries of *The Ashley Book of Knots*[43] which does for the modern world what we could wish Heraklas, or some other cultivated Greek, had done for the ancient world. For Heraklas tells us just enough to prove that the ancients—maritime people like ourselves—were exceedingly adept in the use of man's age-old tool the practical, utilitarian knot.

Notes

CHAPTER I

1. Herodotus, IV. 97-98 (Godley's translation).
2. Karl Weule, *Native Life in East Africa*, tr. Alice Werner, 1909, p. 328.
3. Thomas Shaw, *On the Inhabitants of the Hills near Rajamahall*, 1795. Cited by Locke, *The Ancient Quipu*, 1923, p. 62.
4. Edgar Thurston, *Ethnographic Notes in Southern India*, 1906, p. 13.
5. F. W. Hodge, *Handbook of American Indians North of Mexico*, II (1912), 281 and 319, *s. v.* "Pope" and "Pueblos."
6. *The Discoveries of John Lederer* (1671), ed. W. P. Cumming, 1958, pp. 12-13.
7. *Lawson's History of North Carolina* (1714), ed. F. L. Harris, 1937 and 1951, p. 40.
8. James Adair, *The History of the American Indians*, 1775, p. 75.
9. Carl Lumholtz, *Unknown Mexico*, II (1902), 128.
10. Leslie Spier, *Havasupai Ethnography*, Anthropological Papers of the American Museum of Natural History, 1928, p. 169.
11. J. D. Leechman and M. R. Harrington, *String Records of the Northwest*, 1921, pp. 5-63.
12. Richard Thurnwald, *Forschungen auf den Salomo-Inseln und dem Bismarck-Archipel*, I (1912), 331.
13. C. S. Stewart, *A Visit to the South Seas*, I (1831), 334-335.
14. George Keate, *An Account of the Pelew Islands*, 1789, pp. 160, 230, 245.
15. W. H. Prescott, *History of the Conquest of Peru*, I (1883), 124.
16. Paul Clavérie, *Pages Détachées*, 1884, p. 185.
17. Karl von den Steinen, *Die Marquesaner und ihre Kunst*, II (1928), 64-66, and III (1928), Plate Alpha Gamma.
18. George Turner, *Samoa a Hundred Years Ago*, 1884, p. 302.
19. Daniel Tyerman and George Bennet, *Journal of Voyages and Travels*, ed. Montgomery, II (1832), 71-72.
20. Carl Lumholtz, *Unknown Mexico*, II (1902), 129-130.
21. *Proceedings of the Asiatic Society of Bengal*, 1872, p. 192. Cited by D. E. Smith, *History of Mathematics*, II (1925), 195
22. A. L. Kroeber, *The Arapaho*, The American Museum of Natural History, Bulletin 18, 1902-1907, pp. 199-200.
23. Edmund Simon, "Über Knotenschriften und ähnliche Knotenschnüre der Riukiu-Inseln," *Asia Major*, II (1924), 657-667.
24. *Laotzu's Tao and Wu-Wei*, tr. B. Wai-Tao and B. Goddard, 1939, p. 68.
25. Florian Cajori, *A History of Mathematical Notations*, I (1928), 43.
26. D. E. Smith, *History of Mathematics*, I (1923), 139.
27. J. B. Labat, *Voyage du Chevalier des Marchais en Guinée*, II (1730), 323.
28. S. Gandz, "The Knot in Hebrew Literature, or from the Knot to the Alphabet," *Isis*, XIV, No. 43 (1931), 189-214.
29. *Ibid.*
30. Edmund Simon, "Über Knotenschriften und ähnliche Knotenschnüre der Riukiu-Inseln," *Asia Major*, II (1924), 657-667.
31. Winifred Blackman, Hastings' *Encyclopaedia of Religion and Ethics*, X (1919), 847-856, *s. v.* "Rosaries."

32. *The Incas of Pedro de Cieza de León*, tr. de Onis, 1959, p. 174.

33. Garcilaso de la Vega, *The Royal Commentaries of the Inca*, ed. Gheerbrandt, tr. Jolas, 1961, p. 159.

34. L. L. Locke, "The Ancient Quipu, a Peruvian Knot Record," *American Anthropologist*, New Series, XIV, No. 2 (1912), 325-332.

35. R. A. Altieri, "Sobre 11 Antiguos Kipu Peruanos," *Revista del Instituto de Antropologia*, Tucuman, II, No. 8 (1941), 177-211.

36. C. R. di Primeglio, "Introduccion al Estudio de los Quipus," *Documenta: Revista de la Sociedad Peruana de Historia*, Lima, 1949-1950, pp. 244-339.

37. L. L. Locke, *The Ancient Quipu or Peruvian Knot Record*, 1923.

38. Erland Nordenskiöld, *The Secret of the Peruvian Quipus* and *Calculations with Years and Months in the Peruvian Quipus*, Comparative Ethnographical Studies, Göteborg, VI (1925), Parts 1 and 2.

39. Garcilaso de la Vega, *The Royal Commentaries of the Inca*, ed. Gheerbrandt, tr. Jolas, 1961, pp. 34-38.

40. Felipe Huaman Poma de Ayala, *La Nueva Corónica y Buen Gobierno*, Paris, 1936, pp. 883-885.

41. L. L. Locke, "A Peruvian Quipu," Contributions from the Museum of the American Indian Heye Foundation, VII, No. 5 (1927), 1-11. Locke's schematic diagram of Quipu 14-3866, tipped into this article, contains four errors. His table of values on pp. 7-11 is accurate except that Cord 2 in Group H has a 6-fold long knot instead of a 5-fold long knot. There is a single knot near the end of Summation Cord G. Locke disregards it, and (being unable to account for it) I do not show it in my diagram on p. 28.

42. L. L. Locke, "Supplementary Notes on the Quipus in the American Museum of Natural History," Anthropological Papers of the American Museum of Natural History, XXX, Part 2 (1928), 37-73. Locke's readings of these quipus, especially the larger ones, contain many errors.

43. See footnote 41.

44. Nordenskiöld, *The Secret of the Peruvian Quipus*, 1925, p. 35.

45. G. S. Hawkins, *Stonehenge Decoded*, 1965, pp. 138-143, 176-179.

46. *Ibid.*, p. 178.

47. Garcilaso de la Vega, *The Royal Commentaries of the Inca*, ed. Gheerbrandt, tr. Jolas, 1961, pp. 34-36.

48. Felipe Huaman Poma de Ayala, *La Nueva Corónica y Buen Gobierno*, Paris, 1936, pp. 883-885.

49. Henry Wassén, "The Ancient Peruvian Abacus," *Comparative Ethnographical Studies*, Göteborg, IX (1931), 191-205.

50. Henry Wassén, "El Antiguo Abaco Peruano según el Manuscrito de Guaman Poma," *Etnologiska Studier*, Göteborg, XI (1940), 1-30.

51. Felipe Huaman Poma de Ayala, *La Nueva Cronica y Buen Gobierno*, Lima, 1956, p. 270.

52. L. L. Locke, "The Ancient Peruvian Abacus," *Scripta Mathematica*, I (September, 1932), 36-43.

53. Garcilaso de la Vega, *The Royal Commentaries of the Inca*, ed. Gheerbrandt, tr. Jolas, 1961, pp. 158-159.

54. *Ibid.*, p. 160.

55. Nordenskiöld, *The Secret of the Peruvian Quipus*, 1925, p. 36.

CHAPTER II

1. E. B. Tylor, *Primitive Culture*, 1871; Sir J. G. Frazer, *The Golden Bough*, Volumes I and II ("The Magic Art"), 1911; R. R. Marett, *The Threshold of Religion*, 1900; H. Hubert and M. Mauss, "Esquisse d'une Théorie Générale de la Magie," *L'Année Sociologique*, Volume VII,

1902-1903; K. T. Preuss, *Die geistige Kultur der Naturvölker*, 1914; A. G. L. Lehmann, *Aberglaube und Zauberei*, 1898; R. H. Lowie, *Primitive Religion*, 1924; B. Malinowski, *Argonauts of the Western Pacific*, 1922.

2. F. K. Smith, Hastings' *Encyclopaedia of Religion and Ethics*, VIII (1916), 279, *s. v.* "Magic (Greek and Roman)." The abbreviation *ERE* is used in subsequent citations of Hastings' *Encyclopaedia*.

3. W. J. Dilling, *ERE*, VII (1915), 747-748, *s. v.* "Knots."

4. W. Crooke, *Religion and Folklore of Northern India* [1926], p. 74.

5. *The Odyssey*, Book X.

6. Sir J. G. Frazer, *The Golden Bough* ("The Magic Art"), I (1911), 325.

7. Ranulph Higden, *Polychronicon*, tr. John Trevisa, ed. Babington, II (1869), 41-43.

8. Thomas Nash, *A Pleasant Comedie, Called Summers Last Will and Testament*, 1600.

9. Thomas Nash, *The Terrors of the Night; or, a Discourse of Apparitions*, 1594.

10. Olaus Magnus, *A Compendious History of the Goths, Swedes, & Vandals*, 1658, p. 47. First published in 1555.

11. Viktor Rydberg, *Fädernas Gudasaga*, p. 80. Quoted by Öhrvall, *Om Knutar*, 1916, p. 199.

12. Giles Fletcher, *The Russe Commonwealth*, 1588, in Hakluyt's *Collection of the Early Voyages . . . of the English Nation*, I (1809), 555.

13. Knud Leems, *An Account of the Laplanders*, 1767, in John Pinkerton's *General Collection of the Best and Most Interesting Voyages and Travels*, I (1808), 471.

14. Richard Eden, "Of the North Regions," *The Decades of the Newe Worlde*, 1555, p. 272.

15. Peder Claussøn Friis, *Norriges og Omliggende Øers*, 1727, p. 128.

16. Sir J. G. Fraser, *The Golden Bough* ("The Magic Art"), I (1911), 325.

17. *Ibid.*

18. R. C. Thompson, *The Devils and Evil Spirits of Babylonia*, II (1904), 85.

19. *Ibid.*, p. xii.

20. R. C. Thompson, *Semitic Magic*, 1908, p. 165.

21. S. Seligmann, *Der böse Blick*, I (1910), 262.

22. A. Wuttke, *Der deutsche Volksaberglaube der Gegenwart*, ed. Meyer, 1900, pp. 328-329.

23. W. G. Black, *Folk-Medicine*, 1883, p. 38.

24. Sir J. G. Frazer, *The Golden Bough* ("The Scapegoat"), IX (1913), 57.

25. W. Crooke, *Religion and Folklore of Northern India* [1926], p. 306.

26. C. G. and B. Z. Seligmann, *The Veddas*, 1911, p. 197.

27. J. Spieth, *Die Religion der Eweer*, 1911, p. 50.

28. S. Seligmann, *Der böse Blick*, I (1910), 262.

29. M. A. Owen, *Folk-Lore of the Musquakie Indians*, 1904, p. 111.

30. J. G. Bourke, *The Medicine-Men of the Apache*, Ninth Annual Report of the Bureau of Ethnology, Washington, 1892, pp. 550-580.

31. J. Walker, *Folk Medicine in Modern Egypt*, 1934, p. 43.

32. R. C. Thompson, *Semitic Magic*, 1908, p. 170.

33. *Ibid.*, p. 171.

34. Pliny, *Natural History*, XXVIII.i.5, ix.42,47, xii.48, xxvii.93,94, lxi.218; and XXX.xxx.101.

35. *The Egyptian Expedition 1921-1922*, Part II of the Bulletin of the Metropolitan Museum of Art, December, 1922, p. 35.

36. N. Annandale and H. C. Robinson, *Fasciculi Malayensis*, II (1904), 48-49.

37. O. Schrader, *ERE*, III (1911), 466, *s. v.* "Charms and Amulets (Slavic)."

38. S. Gandz, "The Knot in Hebrew Literature, or from the Knot to the Alphabet," *Isis*, XIV, No. 43 (1931), 192.

39. *Ibid.*

40. *Ibid.*

41. A. C. Kruyt, "'Het Leggen van een Knoop in Indonesie," *Mededeelingen der Koninklijke Akademie van Wetenschappen*, LXXXIV, Ser. B, No. 4 (1937), 150.

42. On amuletic hieroglyphs, see F. W. von Bissing, "Ägyptische Knoten Amulette," *Archiv für Religionswissenschaft*, VIII, Beiheft (1905), 23-26; Sir. E. A. W. Budge, *Amulets and Superstitions*, 1939, p. 128; and Sir Alan Gardiner, *Egyptian Grammar*, third edition, 1964, pp. 74, 239, 508, 523.

43. Lucretius, *De Rerum Natura*, I.930-931.

44. A. Erman, *Die Ägyptische Religion*, 1934, p. 311, No. 128.

45. W. M. F. Petrie, *Amulets*, 1914, Plates XVII, XVIII, XIX.

46. Howard Carter, *The Tomb of Tut-Ankh-Amen*, II (1963), 122, and Plate LXXXIII (A).

47. J. J. M. de Morgan, *Fouilles à Dahchour*, 1895, Plates XV, XVI.

48. H. E. Winlock, *The Treasure of El Lāhūn*, 1934, p. 55, and Plates IX, XII, XIII.

49. Pliny, *Natural History*, XXVIII.xvii.63-64.

50. Sextus Pompeius Festus, *Der Verborum Significatione*, III, *s. v.* "Cingulo" and "Cinxiae Junonis."

51. M. A. Murray, "Knots," *Ancient Egypt*, I (1922), 14-19.

52. H. Schliemann, *Mycenae*, 1878, p. 242, Fig. 352.

53. Sir Arthur Evans, *The Palace of Minos*, I (1921), 430-435.

54. M. P. Nilsson, *The Minoan-Mycenaean Religion*, 1927, pp. 137-138.

55. Hjalmar Öhrvall, *Om Knutar*, 1916, pp. 32, 33, 196.

56. W. Skeat, *Malay Magic*, 1900, pp. 432-433.

57. P. Wolters, "Faden und Knoten als Amulett," *Archiv für Religionswissenschaft*, VIII, Beiheft (1905), 1-22.

58. R. C. Thompson, *Semitic Magic*, 1908, p. 171. The importance of wool in ancient magic is exhaustively treated by Jacob Pley in a monograph entitled *De lanae in antiquorum ritibus usu*, 1911.

59. S. Seligmann, *Der böse Blick*, I (1910), 330.

60. G. F. Abbott, *Macedonian Folklore*, 1903, pp. 19, 23, 124, 227.

61. Isidor Scheftelowitz, *Das Schlingen- und Netzmotiv im Glauben und Brauch der Völker*, 1912, p. 41.

62. M. A. Owen, *Folk-Lore of the Musquakie Indians*, 1904, p. 129.

63. W. R. S. Ralston, *The Songs of the Russian People*, 1872, p. 390.

64. Isidor Scheftelowitz, *Das Schlingen- und Netzmotiv im Glauben und Brauch der Völker*, 1912, p. 55.

65. *Ibid.*, p. 57.

66. S. Seligmann, *Der böse Blick*, II (1910), 229.

67. W. Crooke, *The Popular Religion and Folklore of Northern India*, II (1896), 36.

68. Isidor Scheftelowitz, *Das Schlingen- und Netzmotiv im Glauben und Brauch der Völker*, 1912, p. 39.

69. *Ibid.*, p. 43.

70. *Ibid.*, p. 40.

71. J. Spieth, *Die Religion der Eweer*, 1911, p. 228.

72. W. J. Dilling, *ERE*, VII (1915), 751, *s. v.* "Knots."

73. A. Werner, *The Natives of British Central Africa*, 1906, pp. 80-81.

74. Isidor Scheftelowitz, *Das Schlingen- und Netzmotiv im Glauben und Brauch der Völker*, 1912, p. 43.

75. S. Seligmann, *Der böse Blick*, II (1910), 95, 228.

76. A. C. Kruyt, "Het Leggen van een Knoop in Indonesie," *Mededeelingen der Koninklijke Akademie van Wetenschappen*, LXXXIV, Ser. B, No. 4 (1937), 154.

77. *Ibid.*, pp. 149-150.

78. *Ibid.*, p. 151.

79. *Ibid.*, pp. 153-154.

80. J. G. Dalyell, *The Darker Superstitions of Scotland*, 1834, p. 307.

81. E. Schiller, *Shinto*, 1911, p. 68.

82. W. R. S. Ralston, *The Songs of the Russian People*, 1872, p. 388.

83. Knud Leems, *An Account of the Laplanders*, 1767, in John Pinkerton's *General Collection of the Best and Most Interesting Voyages and Travels*, I (1808), 471.

84. Sir J. G. Fraser, *The Golden Bough* ('Taboo"), III (1911), 301-302.

85. *Ibid.*

86. A. Wuttke, *Der deutsche Volksaberglaube der Gegenwart*, ed. Meyer, 1900, p. 111.

87. Isidor Scheftelowitz, *Das Schlingen- und Netzmotiv im Glauben und Brauch der Völker*, 1912, pp. 11-15.

88. S. Seligmann, *Die Zauberkraft des Auges*, 1922, p. 341 n.

89. J. G. Bourke, *The Medicine Men of the Apache*, Ninth Annual Report of the Bureau of Ethnology, Washington, 1892, p. 567.

90. W. J. Dilling, *ERE*, VII (1915), 749, *s. v.* "Knots."

91. Hjalmar Öhrvall, *Om Knutar*, 1916, p. 200.

92. J. G. Dalyell, *The Darker Superstitions of Scotland*, 1834, pp. 302-307.

93. King James I, *Daemonologie*, 1597, ed. Harrison, 1924, p. 12.

94. J. G. Dalyell, *The Darker Superstitions of Scotland*, 1834, pp. 306-307.

95. Snorri Sturleson, *The Heimskringla*, tr. Laing, ed. Anderson, III (1906), 879-880.

96. R. C. Thompson, *The Devils and Evil Spirits of Babylonia*, I (1904), xxxvii.

97. J. G. Dalyell, *The Darker Superstitions of Scotland*, 1834, p. 307.

98. S. Gandz, "The Knot in Hebrew Literature, or from the Knot to the Alphabet," *Isis*, XIV, No. 43 (1931), 194.

99. Sir J. G. Frazer, *The Golden Bough* ("Taboo"), III (1911), 299-300.

100. Hjalmar Öhrvall, *Om Knutar*, 1916, p. 200.

101. R. C. Thompson, *Semitic Magic*, 1908, p. 170.

102. F. J. Child, *The English and Scottish Popular Ballads*, I (1896), No. 6, pp. 85-87.

103. Pliny, *Natural History*, XXVIII xvii 59.

104. Ovid, *Metamorphoses*, IX.281-315.

105. Pliny, *Natural History*, XXVIII ix.42 (Holland's translation, 1634, p. 301).

106. Virgil, *Eighth Eclogue* (Dryden's translation).

107. Act II, scene ii.

108. *The Connoisseur*, February 20, 1755, No. 56.

109. Hjalmar Öhrvall, *Om Knutar*, 1916, pp. 212-224.

110. F. W. von Bissing, "Ägyptische Knotenamulette," *Archiv für Religionswissenschaft*, VIII, Beiheft (1905), 23-26.

111. Hjalmar Öhrvall, *Om Knutar*, 1916, p. 198.

112. J. J. Modi, *ERE*, VIII (1916), 456, *s. v.* "Marriage (Iranian)."

113. W. J. Dilling, *ERE*, VII (1915), 748-749, *s. v.* "Knots."

114. A. R. S. Kennedy, *ERE*, III (1911), 440, *s. v.* "Charms and Amulets (Hebrew)."

115. W. O. E. Oesterley, *ERE*, II (1910), 327, *s. v.* "Badges."

116. S. Gandz, "The Knot in Hebrew Literature, or from the Knot to the Alphabet," *Isis*, XIV, No. 43 (1931), 197.

117. W. Crooke, *ERE*, III (1911), 444, *s. v.* "Charms and Amulets (Indian)," and W. J. Dilling, *ERE*, VI (1914), 228, *s. v.* "Girdle."

118. W. J. Dilling, *ibid.*, p. 227.

119. W. G. Walshe, *ERE*, IV (1912), 453, *s. v.* "Death and Disposal of the Dead (Chinese)."

120. W. Crooke, *ERE*, III (1911), 444, *s. v.* "Charms and Amulets (Indian)."

121. W. S. Blackman, *ERE*, X (1919), 855, *s. v.* "Rosaries."

122. The Metropolitan Museum of Art, Rogers Gift, 1924, No. 34.122.

123. J. G. Bourke, *The Medicine Men of the Apache*, Ninth Annual Report of the Bureau of Ethnology, Washington, 1892, p. 557.

124. F. Heckmann, *The Catholic Encyclopedia*, IV (1913), 357-358, *s. v.* "Cord."

125. J. G. Bourke, *The Medicine Men of the Apache,* Ninth Annual Report of the Bureau of Ethnology, Washington, 1892, p. 557.

126. E. Westermarck, *The Origin and Development of the Moral Ideas,* II (1908), 585.

CHAPTER III

1. J. E. Lips, *The Origin of Things,* 1947, p. 122.

2. Fragments of a Mesolithic fish net, probably a knotless net, and thought to date from about 6850 B. C., were found a half a century ago in a Finnish peat bog. Fish nets of a much later date, together with quantities of thread, string, and rope, were found in the nineteenth century when a drought uncovered some of the sites of the habitations of the Neolithic Swiss Lake Dwellers. The Lake Dwellers, who were excellent weavers and cordage makers, used the weaver's knot (or sheet bend) as a mesh knot. Cf. J. G. D. Clark, *The Mesolithic Settlement of Northern Europe,* 1936, p. 109; Ville Lubo, *Porin Verkkoloyto,* 1954, *passim;* F. Keller, *The Lake Dwellings of Switzerland,* I (1878), 506-510; Robert Munro, *The Lake Dwellings of Europe,* 1890, p. 114; H. F. Cleland, *Our Prehistoric Ancestors,* 1928; and J. G. D. Clark, *Prehistoric Europe,* 1952.

3. Lashings, technically, are a kind of knot. The Gordian knot, for example, was a lashing. Turk's head knots are "decorative" lashings (see the diagram on page 83). They were much admired by nineteenth-century mariners.

4. The nautical purist distinguishes two kinds of hitches: the single hitch and the half hitch. The hitch that secures the last turn of a lashing is a single hitch.

5. The overhand knot is not only elementary but elemental. The *Leucothrix mucor,* a colorless, macroscopic, filamentous marine bacterium of the algae family, ties itself into overhand knots in the course of its development, and even sometimes into figure-eight knots and timber hitches. See T. D. Brock, "Knots in Leucothrix mucor," *Science,* CXLIV, No. 3620 (May 15, 1964), 870-873. The cover of this issue of *Science* is given over to diagrams of the knots in question.

The hagfish, another elementary organism, also ties itself into knots. The hagfish is called the slime eel by fishermen and is related to the blood-sucking lamprey. It is practically blind, lacks jaws and stomach, feeds on dead fish, and defends itself when threatened by exuding a thick slime which predatory fish find repulsive. To cleanse itself of this suffocating slime, it ties an overhand knot in its tail and then rubs the slime away by "rolling itself" through the knot from its tail to its head. It ties itself into a knot, also, in order to escape capture and to apply leverage to the objects it feeds on. See David Jensen's summary of the results of his research in *The Scientific American,* CCXIV, No. 2 (February, 1966), 82-90, and Thomas Prentiss's vivid colored painting of the knotted fish on the cover of the same issue of the magazine.

6. Ivan Sanderson (*Animal Treasure,* 1937, p. 187) says that gorillas tie granny knots in saplings and creepers, and occasionally square knots (by chance, of course), when making their nests. He was probably pulling his readers' legs, however, for G. B. Schaller (*The Mountain Gorilla,* 1963, p. 188) reports that there was "no interlacing, weaving, knot-tying, or other involved manipulation" in any of the numerous nests he and his wife examined in 1959-1961. Attempts to teach chimpanzees and organgutans to tie knots have been unsuccessful, but a female chimpanzee learned to thread a needle in 1917 (R. M. and A. W. Yerkes, *The Great Apes,* 1929, pp. 183, 327).

7. I have been unable to learn anything very specific about the attitude of primitive people toward the square knot. The ancient Egyptians, Greeks, and Romans were well aware of its superiority to the granny.

8. Tom Bowling (pseudonym) appears to have given this knot the name lark's head (*A Book of Knots,* 1866). An older name, and probably a more authentic one, is cow hitch.

9. The overhand loop knot is the simplest and most natural way to tie a permanent loop in a thread, string, or rope. It is sometimes called the thumb knot. The bowline knot serves the

same purpose. I have been unable to find any proof that the bowline is an ancient knot, but I suspect that the Egyptians, Greeks, and Romans knew it.

10. The overhand slip knot, also called merely the slip knot, is the most obvious and elementary knot to use as a snare.

11. The weaver's knot can be tied by several different manual techniques, and it has several other names, including sheet bend, becket bend, signal halyard bend, swab hitch, and simple bend.

12. Gilbert Wilson, *The Horse and the Dog in Hidatsa Culture*, Anthropological Papers of the American Museum of Natural History, XV, Part 2 (1924), *passim*.

13. Clark Wissler, *Material Culture of the Blackfoot Indians*, Anthropological Papers of the American Museum of Natural History, V (1910), 99-114.

14. Ralph Linton, *The Material Culture of the Marquesas Islands*, Memoirs of the B. P. Bishop Museum, VIII, No. 5 (1923), 380.

15. Ralph Linton, *ibid.*; P. H. Buck, *Ethnology of Tongareva*, B. P. Bishop Museum Bulletin 92, 1933, and *Arts and Crafts of the Cook Islands*, B. P. Bishop Museum Bulletin 179, 1944; W. C. Handy, *Handcrafts of the Society Islands*, B. P. Bishop Museum Bulletin 42, 1947; Bronislaw Malinowski, *Coral Gardens and Their Magic*, 1935.

16. Franz Boas, *The Eskimos of Baffin Land and Hudson Bay*, Bulletin of the American Museum of Natural History, XV (1907), 4, 28, 34-41, 82-85.

17. A possible way of tying the Eskimo bowline is to pass the end of the thong round an object that is *in front of you*, and then to use the Boy Scout "squirrel-round-the-tree-and-into-the-hole" technique. If this is the way the Eskimos tied it, they probably learned the knot from European sailors.

18. The fisherman's loop knot, or true-lover's knot, is especially well adapted for use in slippery rawhide thongs. The Point Barrow Eskimos were using it in the 1880's (see John Murdoch, *Ethnological Results of the Point Barrow Expedition*, Ninth Annual Report of the Bureau of Ethnology, Washington, 1892, p. 279), and I surmise that it is a genuine Eskimo knot. Heraklas described it in the first century A.D. See Appendix B, below.

19. W. F. Edgerton, "Ancient Egyptian Ships and Shipping," *Journal of Semitic Languages and Literatures*, XXXIX (1923), 133. On the rigging of Egyptian ships, see H. E. Winlock, *Models of Daily Life in Ancient Egypt*, 1955, Plates 71, 84, and 85. On nineteenth-century Polynesian "bound" boats, see P. H. Buck, *Ethnology of Tongareva*, Bishop Museum Bulletin 92, 1933, p. 192.

20. Herodotus, VII. 34-36 (Godley's translation).

21. R. W. Macan, *Herodotus*, I (1908), 53-54.

22. Heraklas is believed on linguistic evidence, to have been a pupil or associate of Heliodorus. See Wilhelm Crönert, "Sprachliches zu griechischen Ärzten," *Archiv für Papyrusforschungen und Verwandte Gebiete*, II (1902-1903), 474-482.

23. The Greek text of Oribasius has been definitively edited by J. Raeder (*Oribasii Collectionum Medicarum Reliquiae*, 4 volumes, Leipzig and Berlin, 1928-1933).

24. MS. Latin 6866, fols. 130a-134b.

25. Hjalmar Öhrvall, "Nagot om knutar i antiken särskildt hos Oreibasios," *Eranos*, XVI (1916), 51-81.

26. L. G. Miller, "The Earliest (?) Description of a String Figure," *The American Anthropologist*, XLVII (1945), 461-462.

27. W. E. Roth, *North Queensland Ethnography*, Home Secretary's Department, Brisbane, Bulletin No. 4 (Games, Sports, and Amusements), 1902, Plate X.i.2.

28. The concept of lifting is present in other meanings of the cognates καρχήσιος and καρχήσιον. The former also denotes the halyards of a ship, and the latter (among its five meanings) a crane for unloading a ship.

29. E. Saglio, *Dictionnaire des Antiquités Grecques et Romaines*, III.i.132, s. v. "Himanteligmos."

30. Harry Craigin, *A Boy's Workshop*, 1884, pp. 204-221.

31. Oskar Seyffert, *A Dictionary of Classical Antiquity*, ed. Nettleship and Sandys [1894], p. 488.

32. J. E. Lips, *The Origin of Things*, 1947, p. 144.

33. H. S. Villard, "Rubber-Cushioned Liberia," *The National Geographic Magazine*, XCIII (1948), 226.

34. Raoul Allier, *The Mind of the Savage*, 1929, p. 46.

35. *The Odyssey*, VIII.447.

36. The Gordian knot was a yoke knot that bound the shaft of a chariot at right angles to the yoke. It could, conceivably, have been a sort of Turk's head knot. See page 83 for a diagram of a Turk's head.

37. Karl von den Steinen, *Die Marquesaner und ihre Kunst*, II (1928), 66.

38. *Encyclopedia of Knots*, 1944, p. 526.

39. *The New Yorker*, October, 1944.

40. *The Ashley Book of Knots*, 1944, p. 3.

41. J. M. Drew, "Rope Cordage," in L. Griswold's *Handicraft*, 1942 edition, p. 400.

42. Stanley Barnes, *Anglers' Knots in Gut and Nylon*, 1947, p. 95.

43. *The Ashley Book of Knots*, 1944. It should not be inferred that there are 3,854 different knots. Many of Ashley's entries represent duplicates and alternate forms. In 1627, Captain John Smith, in his *Seaman's Grammar*, said that "the" three knots used by sailors were the "boling" knot, the wall knot, and the sheepshank. The knots on the Swedish warship "Gustavus Vasa," which sank off Stockholm in 1628 and has recently been raised, are now under study. They include a double Matthew Walker knot, which was mistakenly publicized on Swedish TV as a previously unknown knot, but later correctly identified. No further information about the "Vasa's" knots has as yet been released. Diagrams of the bowline, the Matthew Walker, the sheepshank, and the wall knot are provided on page 83, above.

Appendices: Oribasius *De Laqueis*

MANUSCRIPTS, EDITIONS, AND ILLUSTRATIONS

THE OLDEST EXTANT MANUSCRIPT of Oribasius's *Medical Collections* is the Laurentian Library's MS. Plut. 74.7. This "noble" manuscript—the adjective is Raeder's—was made in the tenth century by the Byzantine physician Nicetas, possibly at the command of the Emperor Constantine Porphyrogenitus (905-959). Parts of it are illustrated by colored miniatures, but not the parts, unfortunately, attributed to Heraklas.

The Codex of Nicetas, as MS. Plut. 74.7 is sometimes called, was brought to Italy in the fifteenth century by an eminent Greek scholar, John Lascaris by name, a refugee from Turkish-dominated Constantinople. Cardinal Niccolo Ridolfi, the bibliophile, acquired it, and Vidus Vidius (1500-1569), a Florentine who became physician to Francis I and professor of medicine in the Collège de France, translated it into Latin. Vidius is remembered today, not only because he translated Oribasius, but also because the Vidian nerve, the Vidian canal, and the Vidian artery, which he first described, are named for him.

The manuscript of Vidius's translation (MS. Latin 6866 in the Bibliothèque Nationale) contains about two hundred pen-and-bistre drawings by the Italian painter, sculptor, and architect Francesco Primaticcio (1504-1570), the leading artist in France during the middle years of the sixteenth century. Most of his drawings are modified copies or imitations of the miniatures in the Codex of Nicetas, but at least eighteen of them, illustrative of Heraklas's chapters on surgeon's slings, are new. Only one of the eighteen, the drawing of the *ertos brokhos* (Heraklas's Chapter 1), interprets Heraklas's meaning correctly.

Some impressive woodcuts, based on Primaticcio's drawings—mirror copies of them, in effect—are included in a handsome folio edition of Vidius's translation, sponsored by Francis I, and entitled *Chirurgia e Graeco in Latinum conuersa, Vido Vidio Florentino interprete, cum nonnullis eiusdem Vidii commentariis*, Paris, 1544. These woodcuts are obviously the work of a master, and may be by Primaticcio himself.

Imitations of the woodcuts in Vidius's folio, all of them artistically commonplace, are included in at least three early editions of Oribasius: namely, 1. *Chirurgia. De Chirurgia Scriptores Optimi quique Veteres et Recentiores, Plerique in Germania Antehoc Non Editi*, Zurich, 1555 (folio); 2. *Medicae artis principes, post Hippocratem & Galenum,* Paris, 1567 (2 volumes in 5 parts, folio, edited by Henricus Stephanus, i.e., Henri Estienne, 1528-1598, called "le Grand"); and 3. *Les Anciens et Renommés Aucteurs de la Medicine & Chirurgie,* Lyon, 1555, and Paris, 1634 and 1654 (octavo). The 1555 and 1654 editions, which I have not seen, are listed in the printed catalogue of the Bibliothèque Nationale. The British Museum and the College of Physicians of Philadelphia possess copies of the other works cited in this and the preceding paragraph.

Vidius, in a note on Folio 305 of Latin MS. 6866 prefixed to Heliodorus's chapters in Oribasius's *Medical Collections,* speaks about the effort he has made "to paint and make wooden" the machines described by Heliodorus, and to place them before the eyes of the reader *(ob oculos ponerem, et pingere et lignea conficere studeo).* He uses the first person singular, but does not mean, of course, that he made the drawings and the woodcuts with his own hands. John Santorinos of Rhodes, he says, and Francisco Primaticcio of Bologna, "distinguished painter to the King of France," assisted him.

This note of Vidius's is the only direct evidence, as far as I know, that Primaticcio made the drawings in MS. Latin 6866, and it is for this reason, I suspect, that Henri Omont uses the cautious phrase "attribués au Primatice" on the title-page of his *Collection de Chirurgiens Grecs* [1908], which includes facsimiles of the drawings in the manuscript. Louis Dimier, on the other hand, does not question the attribution in his authoritative *Le Primatice,* 1928.

But if Primaticcio was solely responsible for the drawings in Vidius's manuscript, who was Santorinos, and what was his role in the undertaking? According to Dimier (who does not cite the source of his information), Santorinos was an apothecary, and Primaticcio worked under his direction. Omont, on the other hand, cites a Greek epigram by John Lascaris (who brought the Codex of Nicetas to Italy) in which Santorinos is credited with having made the drawings in MS. Grec 2247 (Bibliothèque Nationale). This manuscript is a copy of the Codex of Nicetas. It does not contain any drawings of Heraklas's knots. Lascaris's epigram can be found in Émile Legrand's *Bibliographie Hellénique,* III (1903), 410.

Somewhat before Vidius's time, and Primaticcio's—probably, in fact, in the fifteenth century—an anonymous artist had tried to identify and depict Heraklas's knots. His drawings, which are in one of the Greek manuscripts of Oribasius in the Bibliothèque Nationale (MS. Grec 2248), are clumsy in comparison with Primaticcio's, and they reveal an even more fundamental misunderstanding of Heraklas's meaning. They are rather charming, however, in a naïve sort of way. Thus, when Heraklas prescribes a noose round a broken bone in a patient's limb, the literal-minded artist draws a picture of a bone—sans flesh, sans skin, sans everything. Vidius and Primaticcio were probably acquainted with his drawings, for their interpretations of Heraklas's Chapters 1, 2, 4, 7, and 18 are identical with his. Only his first diagram, illustrative of the *ertos brokhos,* is correct.

More than four and a half centuries went by before another attempt was made to identify Heraklas's knots, and then, in 1916, Öhrvall published his article "Något om knutar i antiken, särskildt hos Oreibasios" in the Swedish periodical *Eranos.* Bussemaker and Daremberg had included drawings by P. Lackerbauer, purporting to depict Heraklas's knots, in their comprehensive edition of Oribasius (*Œuvres d'Oribase,* 6 volumes, Paris, 1851-1876);[1] but these are mere copies, chosen haphazardly, of the drawings in MS. Grec 2248 and in MS. Latin 6866. Only the first is correct.

Hjalmar Öhrvall was well qualified to understand Heraklas's descriptions. A physiologist with an international reputation, a popular professor in Upsala University, and an experienced yachtsman, he was the author of an excellent knot-book entitled *Om Knutar* (first edition, 1908; second edition enlarged, 1916). Öhrvall's identification of Heraklas's Chapters 2, 5, 7, 8, 9, 10, 11, 13, 14, 17, and 18 are correct, in my opinion, but he goes astray in his interpretations of Chapters 1, 3, 4, 6, 12, 15, and 16. Further comment on his identifications is provided on page 151 in my notes on the individual knots.

The late Lawrence G. Miller of Boston, a man with an analytical turn of mind, became interested in Heraklas's knots and slings during World War II and succeeded in identifying all of them to his own satis-

[1] Raeder's edition of Oribasius (*Oribasii Collectionum Medicarum Reliquiae,* 4 volumes, Berlin, 1928-1933) has superseded Bussemaker and Daremberg's. It does not contain any illustrations.

faction and to mine. He published only one of his identifications himself: the *plinthios* (Heraklas's Chapter 13)—see his article entitled "The Earliest (?) Description of a String Figure" in *The American Anthropologist*, XLVII (1945), 461-462. I included them, however, together with a free translation of Heraklas, based primarily on Bussemaker and Daremberg's French translation, in *The Art of Knotting and Splicing* (Dodd, Mead, 1947; U. S. Naval Institute, 1955). Miller's interest in Heraklas was a by-product of his familiarity, acquired during many years of practice as a patent attorney, with the intricacies of the knot-tying machines that are used in the textile industry.

Vidius's purpose in publishing his translation of Oribasius was to furnish the physicians of his day with useful information about Greek medical lore. Öhrvall and Miller labored over Heraklas's descriptions for their own amusement. I have labored over them because of a quixotic compulsion to finish the things that I begin. The result of my labor, presented in the following pages, is a memorial (definitive, I hope) to the obscure Greek physician named Heraklas and his obscure but fascinating little essay on knots.

CHAPTER I: THE ERTOS BROKHOS

1. How the noose called continuous is tied. From Heraklas.

For the tying of the continuous noose, a cord, folded double, is procured. The ends are held in the left hand, and the loop is placed on the ends with the right hand. Then the slack parts of the cord, that is, the ends, are passed together through the middle of the loop. In this way the knot of the noose is on one side and the ends are on the other.

In its function, this is a noose of unequal tension, and it is useful not only for traction but also for holding a limb during reduction and for placing the body in position during a surgical operation. It has been adapted for traction on limbs with two bones when one of the bones is injured, the loops of the noose being arranged on the injured bone, and the ends on the sound one. The loops, applied close to the skin, pull the injured parts vigorously; the ends, separated from the skin, do not pull the injured parts, or pull them less.

This noose is adapted for holding a limb that is being reduced, as in the three kinds of elbow dislocations, that is, the interior, exterior, and

I. ERTOS BROKHOS

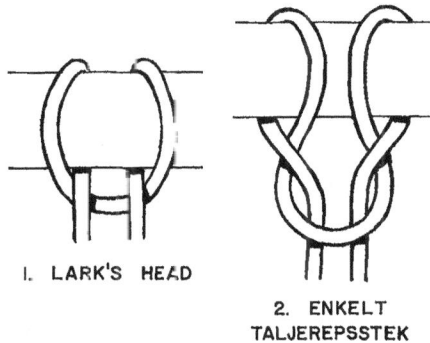

I. LARK'S HEAD

2. ENKELT
TALJEREPSSTEK

posterior kinds, when the arm is bent and cannot be straightened. The noose is placed round the bones of the forearm close to the wrist, and then the ends are carried up and attached to something immovable to hold them. The noose is also useful for holding the body in position during surgery. In ailments of the rectum, the forearms are placed

*under the hams, and continuous nooses are put round the forearms
near the wrists, and then the ends of the nooses are carried up behind
the patient's neck and knotted together.*

*The continuous noose is not only tied before being put round, but
it is also completed while being put round the limb. A cord . . . and
the loop is placed under the limb, and the ends of the cord are passed
together through the middle of the loop. And in this way the noose in
question is produced while being put round.*

The *ertos brokhos* is the easiest of Heraklas's knots to identify. MS.
Grec 2248, MS. Latin 6866 (Vidius and Primaticcio), and Miller agree
that it is the knot commonly seen on keys and baggage tags and called,
in English, the lark's head or cow hitch. Öhrvall alone has doubts and
argues that Heraklas's directions, although they *seem* to produce a
lark's head, actually produce what he calls an *enkelt taljerepsstek*,
which, literally translated, means "single lanyard hitch," and must not
be confused with the *enkelt taljerepsknop*, or Matthew Walker knot.

But Heraklas's directions produce an *enkelt taljerepsstek* only if,
after the loop of the cord is folded back, the ends are separated, carried
past the loop, and then returned through the loop. Heraklas, as I read
him, does not suggest anything of the sort.

Öhrvall appears to have been influenced by Bussemaker and Daremberg, who translate the word ἐρτός by the word *tressé* (braided).
Öhrvall translates it by the Swedish equivalent *snodd* (twisted), and
since the lark's head, as he points out, does not in any way deserve the
name *snodd* knot, he concludes that the *ertos brokhos* is not a lark's
head.

Ἐρτός, however, does not mean *tressé, snodd, braided,* or *twisted.*
Liddell and Scott define it as "threaded, passed through," and derive it
from the verb εἴρω (tie, join, fasten together). They seem to have inferred its meaning from their interpretation of Heraklas's directions as
well as from its etymology. I have translated it by the word "continuous," for εἴρω, which is related to the Latin *sero*, implies a "fastening together in rows," as a string of beads; and the hitches of a lark's
head can be laid on continuously, one after the other, and need not be
limited to two. Vidius calls the *ertos brokhos* a *laqueus attolens*, or
lifting hitch, an appropriate name in view of the universal use of the
knot as a sling for lifting barrels, bales, and other heavy objects.

The word ἐρτός is not a *hapax legomenon,* as the *Thesaurus Graecae Linguae* seems to imply, for Heliodorus, one of Heraklas's contemporaries, uses it twice in his account of the machines used by physicians in the first century A. D. for the purpose of exerting traction and achieving extension in the reduction of disclocations (Oribasius, Book XLIX, Chapters 10 and 30). Primaticcio's drawings of Heliodorus's machines correctly depict the *ertos brokhos* as a lark's head—for example, the drawing on folio 346 of Vidius's manuscript and (as a woodcut) on page 529 of Vidius's 1544 folio.

CHAPTER II: THE NAUTIKOS BROKHOS

2. How the noose called nautical is tied.

A cord is procured, and two loops (placed beside each other according to an opposite arrangement, one of them outside from within, the other inside from without) are tied in the middle of the slack part of the cord. Thus the knot of the noose is on one side and the ends on the other.

This noose, too, is considered useful for exerting unequal tension, and also for holding splints when applying splints to fractures. After the bandaging, the end of the thong is held in the left hand, and with the rest of the slack part, first one loop is made, and then another, round the injured limb. Then the opposite end of the thong is passed through the middle of the loops from the near to the opposite side and held with the left hand. The noose having been formed, the splints are placed round the injured limb between the noose and the bandage, and the ends of the thong are pulled tight and knotted together to hold the splints.

The same noose has been adapted for suspending the forearm as well as for traction and for holding the splints together. It is tied and placed round the forearm when the available bandage is not large enough for the suspension of the arm. The loops of the noose are separated from each other, one loop being placed near the elbow and the other near the wrist, and the ends are carried up round the patient's neck and knotted together.

Both Öhrvall and Miller identify the *nautikos brokhos,* probably correctly, as the familiar mariner's knot called in English the clove hitch. Heraklas describes two ways to tie it, in hand and in situ, and both of his descriptions present problems. To tie it in hand, according to his first description, place two loops beside each other, "one of them outside from within, the other inside from without." These are enigmatical words, to say the least, and they illustrate very well the inadequacy of verbal descriptions of knots unaccompanied by diagrams. My interpretation of what they mean is shown in Fig. 1. Primaticcio and the anonymous artist of MS. Grec. 2248 picture the knot that Öhrvall, in his interpretation of the *ertos brokhos,* calls the *enkelt taljerepsstek.*

Heraklas's description of the way to tie the *nautikos brokhos* in situ (i.e., while putting it round a patient's limb) is clear enough, but

II. NAUTIKOS BROKHOS

1. FIRST METHOD

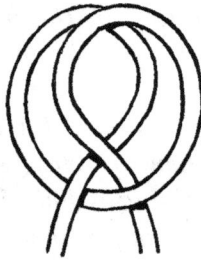

2. CLOVE HITCH FRONT VIEW

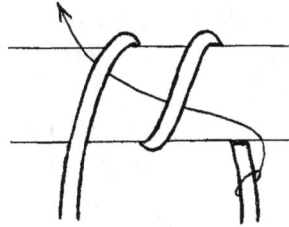

3. SECOND METHOD LITERAL INTERPRETATION

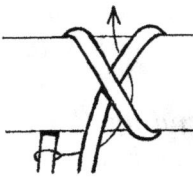

4. SECOND METHOD ALTERNATIVE INTERPRETATION

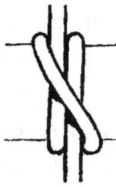

5. CLOVE HITCH SIDE VIEW

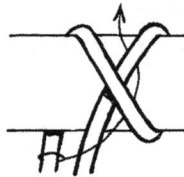

6. SECOND METHOD ANOTHER INTERPRETATION

7. CONSTRICTOR KNOT

nonetheless unsatisfactory. Forming two loops round an object and then passing the end through both loops (see Fig. 3) does *not* produce a clove hitch, or in fact any knot at all. Öhrvall, disturbed by the plural "loops," suggests that Heraklas "without doubt refers to the second loop."

My way out of the difficulty is to assume that the second loop is laid over the first loop (see Fig. 4). This solution to the problem salvages the plural "loops," but does not dispose of all possible doubts.

If the working end is passed *over* the standing part (Fig. 6) instead of *under* it (Fig. 4), the result is the constrictor knot instead of the clove hitch. I am not suggesting that the *nautikos brokhos* is the constrictor knot, but in view of the similarity between the technique of tying it and Heraklas's technique of tying the clove hitch (or at least my interpretation of his technique), it is interesting to speculate if the ancients were familiar with it.

Modern users of knots are *not* generally familiar with it. Indeed, it seems to have been utterly unknown in the English-speaking world until Clifford Ashley (who thought he had originated it) taught it to the Portuguese swordfishermen of New Bedford, gave it the name "constrictor knot," and published it in *The Ashley Book of Knots* (1944). Since then, a great many people have become acquainted with it.

Ashley did not originate it, however, for Martta Ropponen, a Finnish Girl Scout leader, had already published it in her excellent handbook entitled *Solmukirja* (1931). She had never seen it in Finland, she wrote me in 1954, but had learned about it from a Spaniard named Raphael Gaston, who called it a whip knot, and told her it was used in the mountains of Spain by muleteers and herdsmen.

We may take it for granted, I think, that it is a traditional knot, handed down from generation to generation (in Spain, at least, if not elsewhere) ever since Roman times and earlier. Some day, I hope, it will turn up somewhere else—among the Arab fishermen of the Red Sea, perhaps, or on a Greek merchant vessel brought to the surface by a modern under-water archaeologist.

The word Heraklas usually uses for "cord" is καιρία, which Liddell and Scott define as a "tape or cord used for ligatures." In the present chapter, he uses the word ἱμάς, which Liddell and Scott define as "a leathern strap or thong." Whether the καιρίαι were also made of leather is a question that perhaps cannot be answered. Heliodorus generally uses the word καιρία in his treatise on machines (Oribasius, Book XLIX, Chapters 1-35), but in at least one instance (Chapter 22), when discussing a machine invented by Apellides and Archimedes, he uses the word κάλος, which means "rope."

CHAPTER III: THE CHIESTOS BROKHOS

3. How the noose called crossed is tied.

For the tying of the crossed noose, a cord, folded double, is procured, and the ends of the cord are held in the left hand, and the loop is held in the right hand. Then the loop is twisted so that the slack parts of the cord are crossed. Hence the noose is called crossed. After the slack parts of the cord have been crossed, the loop is placed on the crossing, and the lower slack part of the cord is pulled up through the middle of the loop. Thus the knot of the noose is in the middle, with a loop on one side and two ends on the other. This likewise, in function, is a noose of unequal tension.

III. CHIESTOS BROKHOS

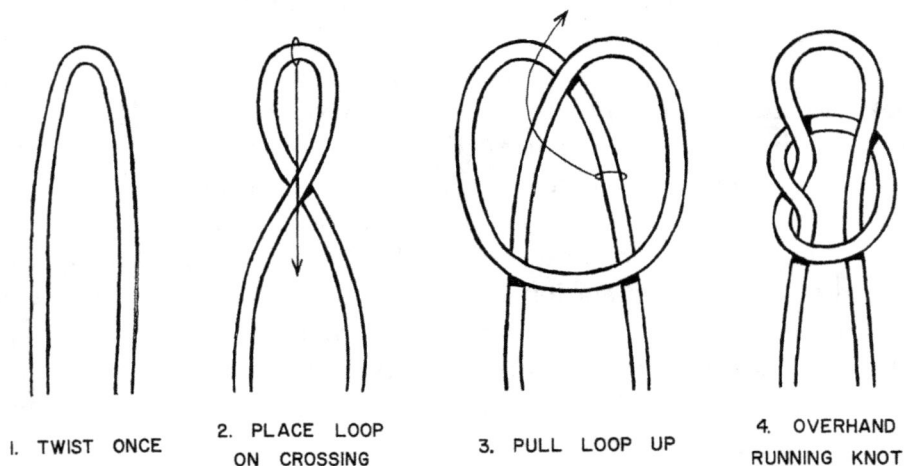

| 1. TWIST ONCE | 2. PLACE LOOP ON CROSSING | 3. PULL LOOP UP | 4. OVERHAND RUNNING KNOT |

The *chiestos brokhos* is undoubtedly our overhand slip knot or running knot. Heraklas's directions, if interpreted literally, seem to produce a mere overhand knot, and Öhrvall so interprets them. It is impossible to believe, however, that anyone as intelligent as Heraklas would tie a mere overhand knot by the involved technique he recommends.

Accordingly, when he says that "the lower slack part is pulled up through the middle of the loop, we must assume that he means a *loop* (or bight) in the lower slack part (Fig. 3), and not the *entire* slack part, end and all.

Öhrvall's interpretation is untenable for two additional reasons: (1) the overhand knot is treated separately in Heraklas's Chapter 6 under the name *haploun hamma* or single knot; and (2) if the *chiestos brokhos* were a mere overhand knot rather than an overhand slip knot, Heraklas's Chapters 4, 15, and 16 would be unintelligible—as, indeed, to Öhrvall they are.

CHAPTER IV: THE SANDALIOS OR BOUKOLIKOS BROKHOS

4. How the noose called pastoral or sandal is tied.

The pastoral noose is also called, by some, the sandal noose. Whatever it may be called by some, it is tied with the so-called crossed noose [Chapter 3]. First tie the crossed noose. Then, so that the sandal noose may be produced, pull the loose loop of the crossed noose up from below through the middle of the loop opposite the ends. Thus the knot of the

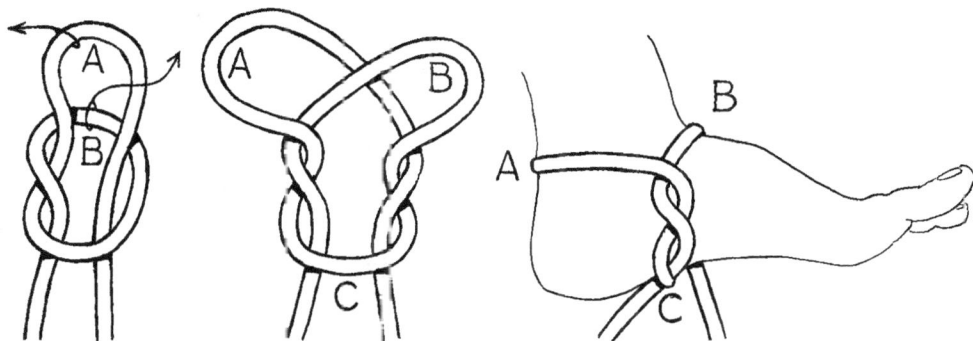

IV. SANDALIOS BROKHOS

1. PULL "A" TO LEFT AND "B" TO RIGHT

2. PUT "A" ON ACHILLES TENDON, "B" ON TARSUS, "C" UNDER SOLE

3. NAMELESS CONSTRUCTION

noose is on one side and the ends on the other. In the knot itself, three loops are seen, two on each side, and the third in the middle.

This noose is useful for extension in the reduction of an ankle. One loop is put round the broad tendon behind the ankle. The second loop is arranged on the front part in the area of the tarsus, and the middle loop, that is, the third, is placed in the area of the sole, and the ends of the noose are then attached to the source of the traction.

This noose is adapted not only for the ankle, but also for the reduction of a dislocated jaw. One loop of the noose is placed on the patient's forehead, a second on the nape of the neck. The middle loop is inserted in the mouth under the jaw, and the ends are carried up past the temples above the patient's head and secured to something to hold them or pull them up.

The *sandalios* or *boukolikos brokhos* should be classified as a sling rather than as a knot or noose. It is an adaptation of the *chiestos brokhos* (Chapter 3), and resembles the modern bandage called Barton's handkerchief or cravat of the heel. See H. R. Wharton's *Minor Surgery and Bandaging*, 3rd edition, 1896, p. 40, Fig. 35. Öhrvall, having failed to identify the *chiestos brokhos* correctly, inevitably goes astray in his interpretation of the *sandalios brokhos*.

CHAPTER V: THE DRAKON BROKHOS

5. How the noose called the serpent is tied.

For the tying of the so-called serpent, the middle is placed on the back of the ankle in the area of the broad tendon. The ends are carried

Ⅴ.   DRAKON BROKHOS

RIGHT: "DOWN FROM ABOVE"
LEFT: "UP FROM BELOW"

past the lateral parts toward the front on the tarsus, and exchanged according to a crosswise arrangement. Then they are carried to the sole of the foot and exchanged again. From the sole they are placed on the turns encircling the ankle, either up from below or down from above, and then they are attached to the source of the traction. This noose is useful for extension in the reduction of a [broken] ankle.

The *drakon brokhos,* like the *sandalios brokhos,* is really a sling rather than a knot or noose. Öhrvall observes that it is impossible to misunderstand Heraklas's directions. Hence he does not provide an illustrative diagram of the *drakon brokhos.* Gerdy's extension knot, illustrated in E. L. Eliason's *Practical Bandaging,* 3rd edition, 1924, Figs. 116B and 116C, is very much like Heraklas's *drakon brokhos.*

CHAPTER VI: THE HAPLOUN HAMMA BROKHOS

6. How the noose called single knot is tied.

The noose called single knot is also called perinaios *by some. Whatever it is called, the knot is considered suitable for the purpose* [for treating the perineum?]. *A cord is procured and a single knot is made in it. Then the loops of the cord are pulled up and the ends allowed to remain free. Then the member to be restored is placed between the upper loops, and one loop is passed through the other loop and carried toward the ends and attached, with a knot shared by the ends, to the source of the traction. In function this also is a noose of unequal tension.*

VI. HAPLOUN HAMMA BROKHOS

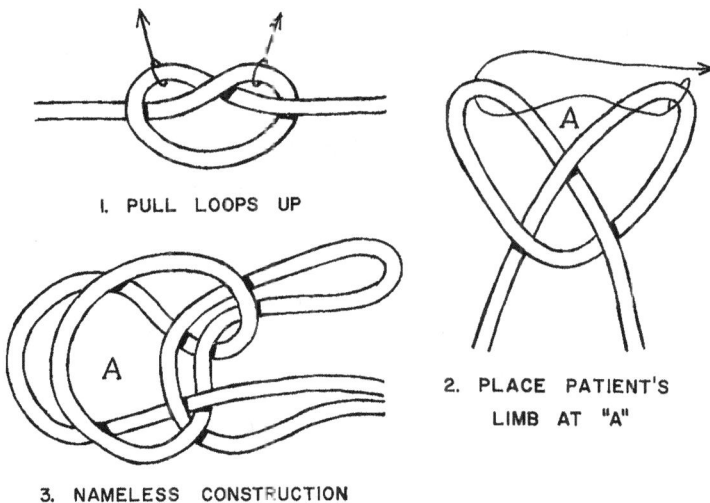

1. PULL LOOPS UP

2. PLACE PATIENT'S LIMB AT "A"

3. NAMELESS CONSTRUCTION

115

Heraklas takes it for granted that his readers will know what he means by a *haploun hamma,* or single knot. Although his directions are for the most part quite clear, it is not self-evident what he means by the loops of a *haploun hamma,* for one does not normally think of an overhand knot as having loops, plural, other than the main loop of the knot. Öhrvall's interpretation of the *haploun hamma brokhos* is incorrect, in my opinion. Miller's interpretation (Figs. 1-3) is much more plausible.

CHAPTER VII: THE LYKOS BROKHOS

7. How the noose called wolf is tied.

Two cords sufficient in length and folded double are procured, and the ends are placed at the same point, and the loops opposite each other. Then the ends of one of the cords are pulled up from below, and those [of the other] are drawn down from above. Thus the knot of the noose appears in the middle, and the two ends on each side. In function this is a noose of equal tension. It is adapted not only for traction in setting bones, but also for binding the peritoneum in the reduction of intestinal hernia, and for binding hemorrhaging vessels.

It is customary for us to hang simple linen cords to the loops of the noose, and most physicians call these cords relaxing cords. We do not use the relaxing cords aimlessly, but in order that, when we wish to relax the ligature, we may do so, not by means of the loops of the noose, but by means of the relaxing cords.

VII. LYKOS BROKHOS

INTERLOOPED BIGHTS

The *lykos brokhos* is structurally identical with the square knot (Heraklas's Chapter 8), but serves to join the bights or middle parts of two cords, whereas the square knot joins the two ends of a single cord.

The distinction is fundamental, and Heraklas, in insisting on it, displays the characteristic acuteness of his intellect. The *skhasteriae*, or relaxing cords, mentioned by Heraklas are attached on each side of the knot and pulled in the directions shown by the arrows in the accompanying sketch.

Heraklas calls the wolf an ἰσότονος noose. The *ertos, nautikos,* and *chiestos brokhoi* (Chapters 1, 2, and 3), he says are ἀνισότονος. These words are not very satisfactorily glossed by Liddell and Scott; and Bussemaker and Daremberg, the French translators of Oribasius, had trouble with them. I have followed their example, however, and used the phrase "of equal (or unequal) tension." I have done so with misgivings, and for lack of a more precise English equivalent.

Heraklas has in mind the fact that some nooses, after being applied to a patient's limb, are intended to be pulled in one direction, or on one side of the limb only. Others, such as the *lykos brokhos,* have ends or loops that have to be pulled on both sides of the limb. Liddell and Scott's definitions of ἰσότονος and ἀνισότονος are "pulling evenly" and "unequally stretched," phrases that are neither grammatically parallel to each other, nor wholly satisfactory in the context of Heraklas's descriptions.

CHAPTER VIII: THE HERAKLEOTIKON HAMMA

8. *How the Hercules knot is tied.*

VIII. HERAKLEOTIKON HAMMA

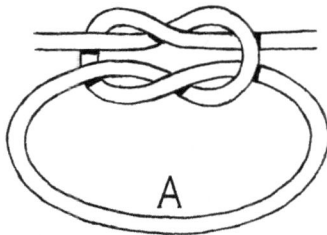

SQUARE KNOT

For the Hercules knot, a cord is procured, and two knots, separated from each other, are formed in this cord. In this way the Hercules knot is produced: a loop on one of the two sides, two ends on the other. This

117

is a noose of equal tension. If we cut the loop in the middle opposite the ends, we find that a wolf [Chapter 7] is produced.

The difference between the *Herakleotikon hamma* and the *lykos brokhos* (Chapter 7), mentioned above, is implicit, I surmise, in the words ἅμμα (knot) and βρόχος (noose). The former suggests a knot that cannot slip, that is pulled tight and remains so. The latter suggests a knot that encloses an object and draws up tighter the harder it is pulled. Heraklas uses the word ἅμμα for one other knot: the *haploun hamma*, or overhand knot, which also remains fixed once it has been pulled tight.

If the cord is cut at point A in the diagram, the result is a *lykos brokhos*, or wolf, as Heraklas observes.

CHAPTER IX: THE HAPLOUS KARKHESIOS

9. *How the single* karkhesios *noose is tied.*

The single karkhesios, *of equal tension in its function, is tied as follows: a cord, folded double, is procured, and the ends are held in the*

IX. HAPLOUS KARKHESIOS

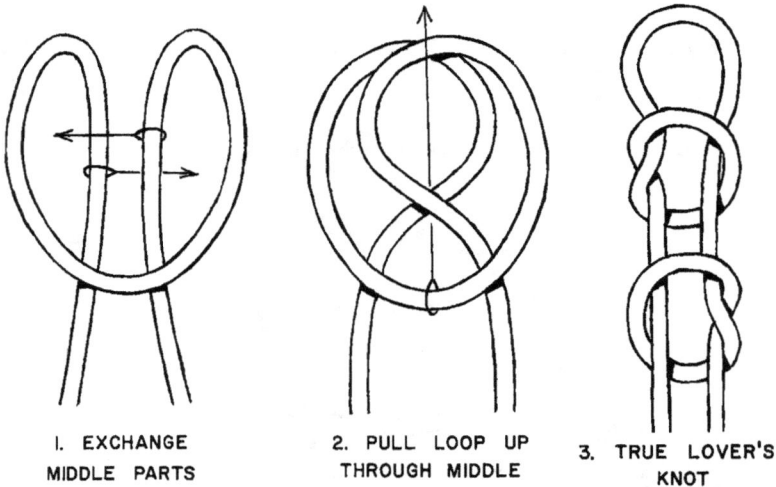

1. EXCHANGE MIDDLE PARTS

2. PULL LOOP UP THROUGH MIDDLE

3. TRUE LOVER'S KNOT

left hand, and the loop, having been folded back with the right hand, is placed on the ends. Then the slack parts of the cord are exchanged in a crosswise fashion, and the loop that has been placed on the ends is pulled down from above through the middle of the crossed parts. Thereupon the knot of the noose is seen in the middle, and a loop on one side and two ends on the other.

The single *karkhesios* is a familiar knot known in every quarter of the globe, and called in English by a variety of names: true-lover's knot, true-love knot, dalliance knot, Englishman's loop knot, fisherman's loop knot, and (among mountain climbers) middleman's knot. Heraklas's directions for tying it are clear and precise, and as a result (or perhaps because everyone in the sixteenth century knew it), one of Primaticcio's drawings is very nearly correct—the one that shows how it looks before being put round a patient's limb. The other drawing, which purports to show it on a man's ankle (see page 137), is an entirely different knot, and bears no resemblance to the true-lover's knot.

This discrepancy is extraordinary, in fact unaccountable from a twentieth-century point of view, but it is not unique. The same sort of pragmatic blindness is revealed in Primaticcio's drawings for Chapters 3, 8, 10, 11, 12, 13, 15, and 16. His drawings for Chapters 10, 11, and 12 (the double *karkhesios*) show six altogether different knots. He was more interested in anatomy, clearly, than in surgeon's slings and nooses.

CHAPTER X: THE DIPLOUS KARKHESIOS (1)

10. How the double karkhesios *is tied.*

With respect to its function, the double karkhesios *is a noose of equal tension, and much more tightly knit than the single* karkhesios *[Chapter 9]. It is tied as follows: A doubled cord is procured, and the ends are held in the left hand, and the loop is allowed to hang free. Then in the opposing slack part of the cord a small loop is tied and placed in the left hand. Through the middle of this little loop the other slack part of the cord is pulled up, and then the knot is turned over by means of the loops and placed in the left hand. Again, the knot having been turned over, another little loop is tied in the opposite slack part of the cord and placed on the knot. Finally the loop that is hanging free is pulled up from below through the middle of the knot. Thereupon, once again, the knot of the noose is found in the middle and a loop on one side and the two ends on the other.*

X. DIPLOUS KARKHESIOS (I)

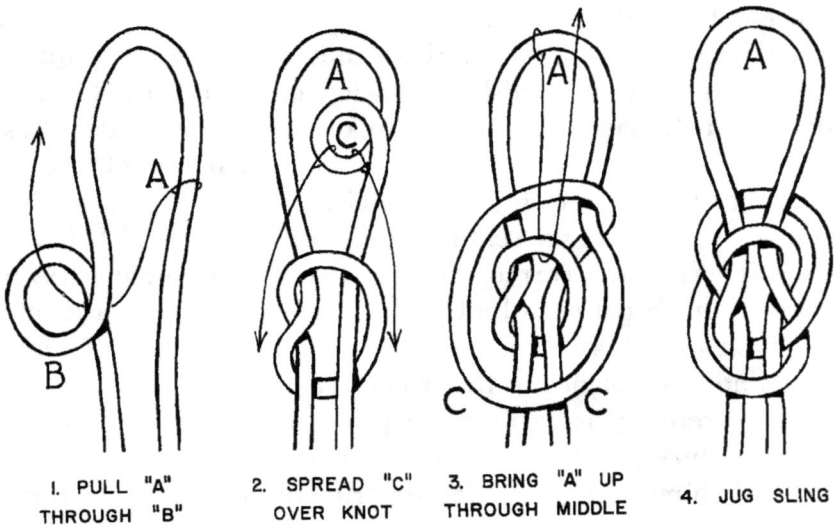

1. PULL "A"
THROUGH "B"

2. SPREAD "C"
OVER KNOT

3. BRING "A" UP
THROUGH MIDDLE

4. JUG SLING

Chapters 10, 11, and 12 show three ways of tying the double *karkhesios;* and all of them produce the ingenious knot known variously as the jug sling, the jar sling, the bottle sling, and the hackamore. The first way is less involved than Heraklas's rather elaborate instructions would seem to indicate, for the starting point in the process is a *chiestos brokhos* (Heraklas's Chapter 3) or overhand running knot.

It is important to note, in following Heraklas's instructions, that he means the middle or bight of the slack part, and not the entire slack part, end and all, when he says that "the other slack part of the cord" is pulled up through the "little loop." The instructions in this chapter, therefore, are exactly like the instructions that troubled Öhrvall in Chapter 3 and led him to identify the *chiestos brokhos* as a mere overhand knot.

Heliodorus, Heraklas's contemporary, prescribes the *karkhesios* "or some other *isotonos* noose" in fifteen of the thirty-five chapters on the machines used by ancient physicians for exerting traction and achieving extension in the reduction of dislocations (Oribasius, Book XLIX, Chapters 8, 9, 10, 12, 13, 17, 21, 24, 25, 28, 29, 30, 31, 33, and 35). He does not say, however, whether he means the single or the double variety of the knot.

Both Primaticcio and Bussemaker and Daremberg assume that he means the single variety. Primaticcio, in his drawings of Heliodorus's machines, always depicts them in the same way that he depicts the single *karkhesios* round a man's ankle in Heraklas's Chapter 9. See page 138 below.

Bussemaker and Daremberg, in their translation of Heliodorus's chapters, provide cross-references to Heraklas's Chapter 9 (the single *karkhesios*), and not to Chapters 10, 11, or 12 (*Œuvres d'Oribase*, IV, 1872, 333-458). It is apparent, however, from Heliodorus's phrase "or some other *isotonos* noose," that either the single *karkhesios* or the double *karkhesios*, or even the *lykos brokhos* (which Heraklas calls a noose of equal tension), would have served his purpose acceptably. Heliodorus and Heraklas themselves, I suspect, used the double *karkhesios*. It is a better knot than the single *karkhesios* (it would hold the patient's limb more securely, and with a more uniformly distributed pressure on the tender skin and flesh), and the fact that Heraklas devotes three chapters to it implies a certain legitimate satisfaction, which Heliodorus probably shared, in knowing how to tie it.

CHAPTER XI: THE DIPLOUS KARKHESIOS (2)

11. How the double karkhesios *is tied from the single* karkhesios.

The double karkhesios *is customarily completed in various ways, sometimes being tied by itself and sometimes from a single* karkhesios. *There is also a way by which it is completed while being put round. Having shown with due regard for reason how it is tied by itself, we now wish to explain how it is brought to completion from a single* karkhesios. *First, therefore, tie the single* karkhesios, *and separate the loops from each other. Then, placing the lower loop on the upper loop, separate the loops from each other and pull the loop that is opposite the ends up from below through the space between the separated loops. In this way, again, the knot of the noose is found to be in the middle, and the two ends on one side and a loop on the other.*

Heraklas's directions for tying the double *karkhesios* from the single *karkhesios* would be difficult to follow if the final result were not known in advance. But Öhrvall and Miller, having solved Chapter 10, find Chapter 11 reasonably intelligible. The chief stumbling block is Hera-

XI. DIPLOUS KARKHESIOS (2)

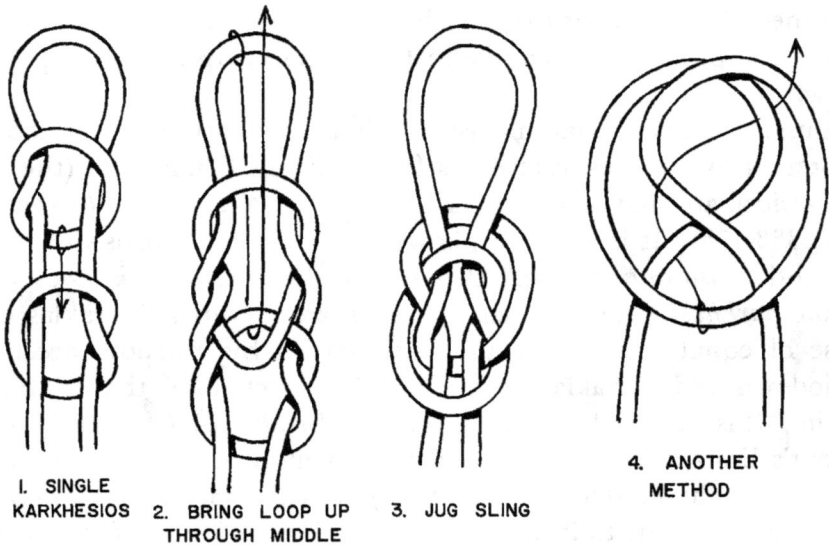

I. SINGLE KARKHESIOS 2. BRING LOOP UP THROUGH MIDDLE 3. JUG SLING 4. ANOTHER METHOD

klas's *second* injunction to separate the loops. These are, in fact, knots rather than loops; and they should be enlarged, so as to overlap, rather than separated. The *overlapping parts* of the loops should be separated, not the loops themselves. See Figs. 1 and 2.

A method of tying the double *karkhesios* not mentioned by Heraklas is shown in Fig. 4 and illustrates the structural relationship between the single and the double *karkhesios*. Compare Fig. 4 on this page and Fig. 2 on page 118. Both methods begin with the same configuration, but, as the arrows show, the loop or bight is passed through the center of the crossed parts in different ways.

CHAPTER XII: THE DIPLOUS KARKHESIOS (3)

12. *How the double* karkhesios *is formed while being put round.*

Since it often happens that the ends of the noose are broken as a result of excessive tension on the taut parts, the traction not yet being ready, we complete the karkhesios *noose as we put it round in order that the ends of the noose that remain free may not be relaxed. We grasp the end of the cord with the left hand, and then, with the slack part, we form three loops round the limb to be set, separated a sufficient distance from each other. After this we place the first loop on the last, and then we pull up the middle loop through the space between them, twisting it once or twice. In this way the knot of the noose is formed round the limb itself, with two ends on one side and a loop on the other.*

XII. DIPLOUS KARKHESIOS (3)

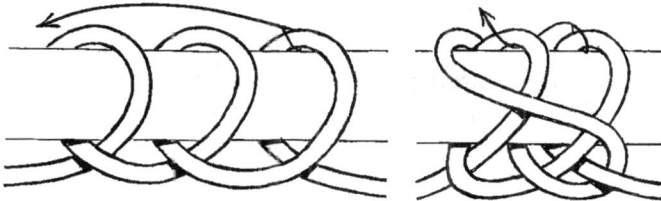

1. "IN SITU"
LITERAL INTERPRETATION

2. RESULT:
SINGLE KARKHESIOS

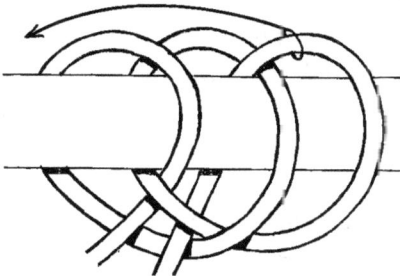

3. "IN SITU"
ALTERNATIVE INTERPRETATION

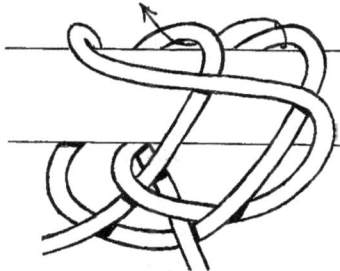

4. RESULT:
DOUBLE KARKHESIOS

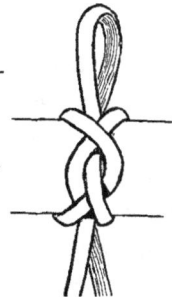

5. JUG SLING
SIDE VIEW

Heraklas's directions for tying the double *karkhesios* round the patient's limb (i.e., in situ) pose a problem. Öhrvall does not attempt to interpret the chapter, and Miller's solution, published in my book *The Art of Knotting and Splicing*, produces an unsatisfactory sort of pseudo-*karkhesios*. Both Öhrvall and Miller postulate a lacuna in the manuscript, and in fact three loops manipulated exactly as Heraklas prescribes seem to produce a single *karkhesios* or true-lover's knot rather than a double *karkhesios*.

This, however, cannot have been Heraklas's intentions, for the single *karkhesios* when tied in the way shown in Figs. 1 and 2 cannot be adjusted and made use of until the object round which it is tied has been removed. There would be no point in tying a single *karkhesios* round a patient's limb by this technique.

I devoted an afternoon to the problem on Washington's Birthday, 1965, and reached the conclusion illustrated in Figs. 3 and 4. As in the case of Heraklas's Chapter 2, where the loops have to be passed round the patient's limb in a particular way in order to produce a *nautikos brokhos* or clove hitch in situ, so here, I believe, the loops prescribed by Heraklas have to be passed round the limb in a particular way in order to produce the double *karkhesios* in situ.

To explain so complicated a procedure verbally would perhaps be an impossibility. One wonders if Heraklas did not rely on diagrams of some sort, and if so why Nicetas did not include them in his codex.

CHAPTER XIII: THE FOUR-LOOP PLINTHIOS

13. How the noose called the four-loop plinthios *is tied.*

For the tying of the plinthios *noose, a cord forming a circle, that is, having no ends, is procured and placed round both hands on the space between the thumb and the little finger. It is also placed round the index finger, so that six loops are produced, three on each hand, on the little finger, on the index finger, and on the thumb. After that the loops are transferred from the thumb to the ring finger and from the little finger to the index finger, and then, with the aid of the thumb, the loops just placed on the index finger are pulled down from above through the space between the first fingers and placed on the index fingers. As a result the knot of the noose appears in the middle in the form of a rhomboid, with two loops on each of the two sides.*

In its function, this is a noose of equal tension, and it seems to be useful not only for extension but also for the setting of fractures of the chin. Sometimes, in fractures of the chin, when we see the fractured parts becoming distorted from the outside, the rhomboidal knot of the noose is placed round the chin, and the loops are carried up past the cheeks and knotted to each other in the area of the top of the head.

The four-loop *plinthios* is as interesting ethnologically as the *karkhesios*. Both Öhrvall and Miller, working independently of each other, equated it with the string figure called "The Sun Clouded Over," which W. E. Roth pictures in his "North Queensland Ethnography,"

XIII. PLINTHIOS BROKHOS

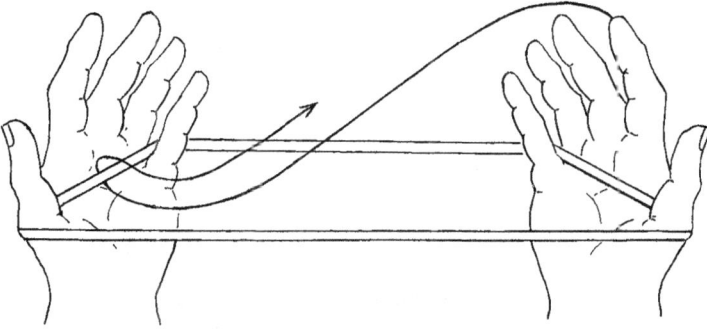

I. POSITION I: PICK LOOPS FROM PALMS WITH INDEX FINGERS

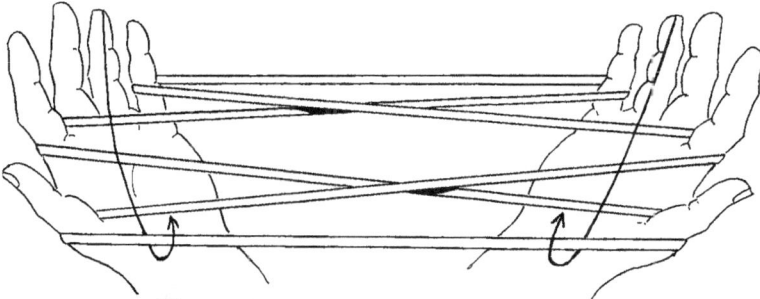

2. OPENING "A": TRANSFER THUMB LOOPS TO RING FINGERS

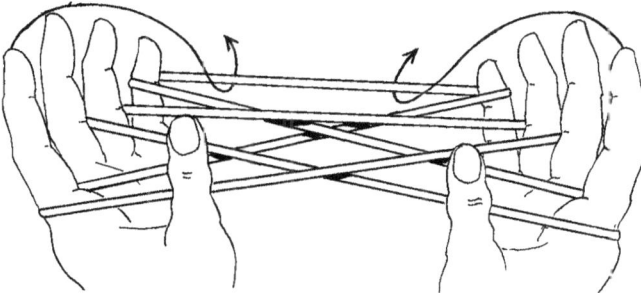

3. TRANSFER LITTLE-FINGER LOOPS TO INDEX FINGERS

1902, Plate X. See Öhrvall's "Något om knutar i antiken, särskildt hos Oreibasios," *Eranos*, XVI (1916), 75-76, and L. G. Miller, "The Earliest (?) Description of a String Figure," *The American Anthropologist*, XLVII (1945), 461-462.

The first part of Heraklas's description coincides with what ethnologists, in their analyses of primitive string figures, call "Position 1" and

125

"Opening A." See Kathleen Haddon's *Artists in String*, n. d., pp. 155-156. Neither Heraklas's nor Miss Haddon's descriptions are unmistakably clear in and by themselves. I have therefore provided five diagrams for the benefit of the neophyte as well as for the reader who has forgotten what he once knew about cat's cradles.

XIII. PLINTHIOS BROKHOS

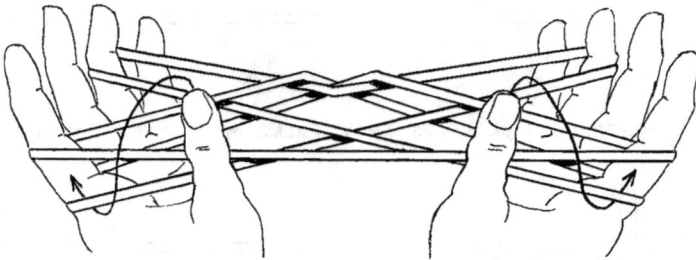

4. WITH THUMBS REMOVE LOWER LOOPS FROM INDEX FINGERS

5. A CAT'S CRADLE: "THE SUN CLOUDED OVER"

The more or less circular pair of loops in the center of the completed figure (Fig. 5) gets smaller and smaller, and finally seems to disappear, when one pulls on the four loops at the corners. Hence the aboriginal name "The Sun Clouded Over," cited by Roth, is extremely apt. And so is the Greek πλίνθιος, for a πλίνθος is a small brick (i.e., a rectangular object), and the word πλινθίον (the diminutive of πλίνθος) denotes any of several square or rectangular objects.

APPENDIX B

CHAPTER XIV: THE EPANKYLOTOS BROKHOS

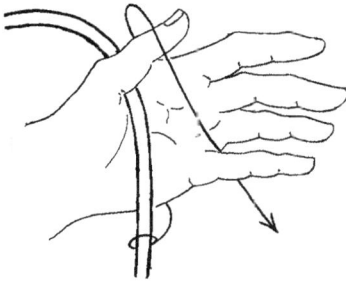

14. How the interlooped noose is tied.

For the tying of the interlooped noose, a cord is procured, and the end is placed on the part of the hand between the thumb and the index finger. The slack part of the cord is rolled round the metacarpus from without, carried to the inner part, placed over the thumb, and held between the little finger and the ring finger. The end is pulled by the right hand, the middle part by the little finger and the ring finger. Thereupon two loops are seen, and between the two loops a running knot. This noose is useful in surgery for placing the body in position. The patient's hands are placed in the loops, and his body is secured by means of the rest of the slack part of the cord.

XIV. EPANKYLOTOS BROKHOS

1. PASS END BACK, OVER THUMB, AND BETWEEN FOURTH AND FIFTH FINGERS

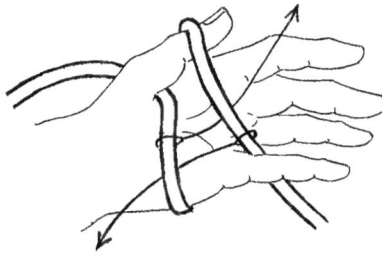

2. PULL ONE LOOP TO LEFT WITH FOURTH AND FIFTH FINGERS, ANOTHER LOOP TO RIGHT WITH RIGHT HAND

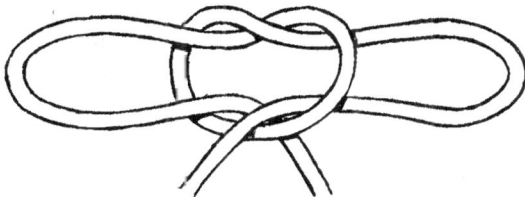

3. TOM FOOL KNOT

The *epankylotos brokhos* is the parlor magician's Tom Fool knot, and Heraklas explains one of the parlor magician's ways of tying it. When he says "the end is pulled by the right hand," he means, of course,

127

a bight or loop in the end, not the whole cord, end and all. Compare his comparable instructions in his descriptions of the *chiestos brokhos* (Chapter 3) and the double *karkhesios* (Chapter 10), which have to be similarily interpreted. Figs. 1 and 2 are intended to make his meaning clear.

The Tom Fool knot can be used to handcuff a prisoner, and it is for the purpose of immobilizing a patient's hands during an operation that Heraklas recommends it.

CHAPTER XV: THE OTA BROKHOS

15. How the noose called the ears is tied.

For the tying of the ears, first tie the noose called interlooped [Chapter 14]. *Make one loop intentionally larger and in it make the crossed noose* [Chapter 3], *in order that two loops may be seen, and that the double slack part of the cord may be found between the two loops.*

This noose is useful for reducing dislocations of the jaw and for articulating the epiphyses of the head. The loops are placed beside the patient's temples, and the double slack part on the forehead between the loops, and then the bandage called the rabbit is put on. After the bandaging the ends of the ears are brought up above the patient's head and attached to something to hold them or to pull them up.

XV.   OTA   BROKHOS

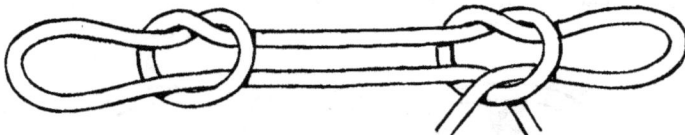

NAMELESS CONSTRUCTION

The *ota brokhos* has no name in English. Öhrvall, having failed to identify the *chiestos brokhos,* or overhand running knot (Chapter 3), is unable to understand the "ears." For it is manifestly impossible to tie an overhand knot (Öhrvall's interpretation of the *chiestos brokhos*) in one of the loops of a Tom Fool knot. It is quite possible, however, to tie an overhand *running* knot in one of the loops of a Tom Fool knot.

The accompanying diagram illustrates Miller's solution to the problem. I have no doubt that it is correct.

The bandage that Heraklas calls the rabbit is described by Heliodorus, Heraklas's contemporary, in Book XLVIII, Chapters 26 and 27, of Oribasius. Heliodorus's name for it is "the rabbit bandage with the ears."

CHAPTER XVI: THE DIANKYLOS BROKHOS

16. How the noose called two-looped is tied (by some incorrectly called the strangler).

The noose called two-looped is made from two crossed nooses [Chapter 3] separated from each other. It is convenient for putting the body in position when treating an ailment of the buttocks. For this purpose, the forearms having been placed under the thighs, the forearms are contained by the crossed nooses. The double slack part of the cord between the nooses is carried up round the patient's neck and in this way the proper position of the body is achieved.

XVI. DIANKYLOS BROKHOS

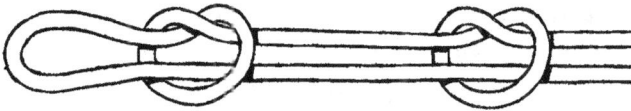

NAMELESS CONSTRUCTION

The *diankylos brokhos* looks very much like the *ota brokhos* (Chapter 15), and has no name in English. Öhrvall, again, fails to solve Chapter 16 because, as in the case of Chapter 15, the solution depends on the correct identification of the *chiestos brokhos* (Chapter 3), which he misconstrues.

CHAPTER XVII: THE ANKHON BROKHOS

17. How the noose correctly called the strangler is tied.

The strangler, correctly so called, is tied with the single karkhesios [Chapter 9]. *A single* karkhesios *is tied, and the loops are separated from each other. It is suitable for the same purposes as the one just described* [Chapter 16]. *The forearms, again, are placed in the loops and bound tightly, and the doubled slack parts of the cord, which are arranged in the middle, are carried up behind the patient's neck.*

XVII. ANKHON BROKHOS

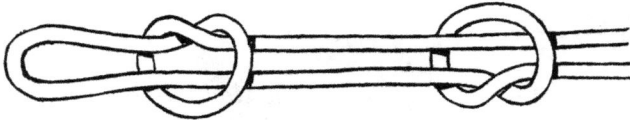

TRUE LOVER'S KNOT

The *ankhon brokhos* resembles both the *ota brokhos* (Chapter 15) and the *epankylotos brokhos* (Chapter 17). It is not a separate, distinct knot, structurally, but rather a single *karkhesios* (Chapter 9) with the two loops or overhand knots arranged at a distance from each other instead of tightly pressed against a patient's limb.

CHAPTER XVIII: THE HYPERBATOS BROKHOS

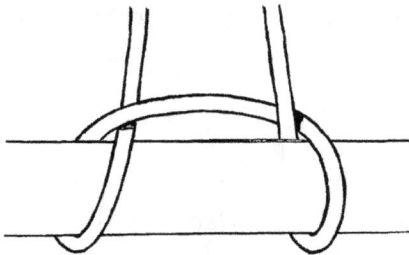

18. How the noose called transposed is tied.

The noose called transposed is made with the noose called nautical [Chapter 2]. *A nautical noose is tied and put round the forearms, and the loops of the noose are separated from each other. The ends are knotted behind the neck.*

And these are the nooses that appear to be useful on a doctor's rounds (διὰ τῆς περιόδου) .

XVIII. HYPERBATOS BROKHOS

CLOVE HITCH

130

Heraklas's *hyperbatos brokhos* is a *nautikos brokhos* or clove hitch (Heraklas's Chapter 2) with the hitches separated. Heraklas explains in Chapter 2 as well as here how to use it as a sling for the forearm. H. R. Wharton, *Minor Surgery and Bandaging*, 3rd edition, 1896, p. 395, pictures a forearm sustained by a clove hitch.

Heraklas's final sentence indicates that his eighteen nooses could be used by themselves as well as in connection with the elaborate machines described by Heliodorus (Oribasius, Book XLIX, Chapters 1-35). Bussemaker and Daremberg render the phrase διὰ τῆς περιόδου as "hors de chez soi."

MS. GREC 2248 C. 1500

ΒΙΒΛΣΙ ΟΥ ΕΚ Τ ΩΝ ΗΡΑΚΛΑ ΠΩΣ ΠΛΕΚΕ ΤΑΙ ΒΡΟΧΟΣ Ο

·ΙΣΟΤΟΝΟΣ· ·ϥΕ·

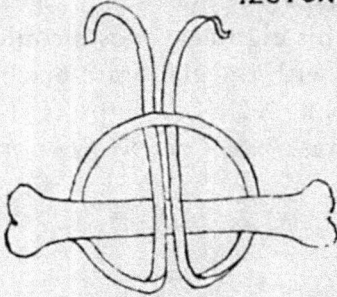

I ERTOS BROKHOS
(CORRECT)

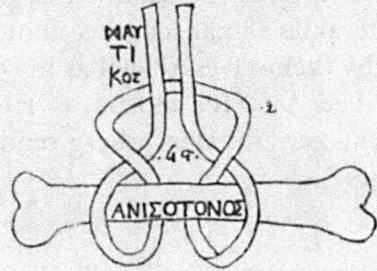

II NAUTIKOS BROKHOS
(INCORRECT)

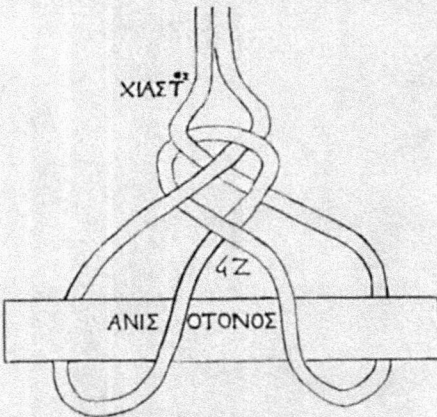

III CHIESTOS BROKHOS
(INCORRECT)

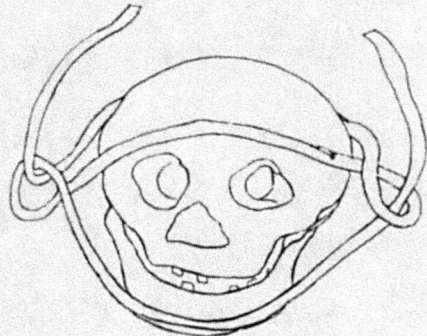

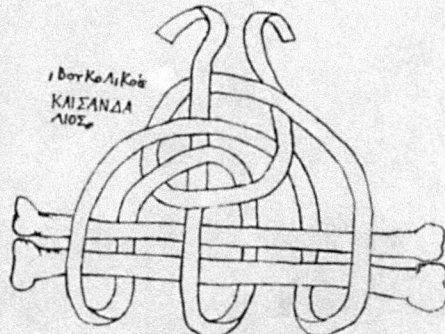

IV SANDALIOS BROKHOS
(INCORRECT)

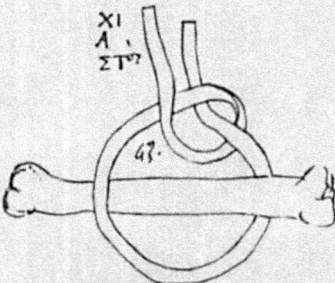

III CHIESTOS BROKHOS
(INCORRECT)

IV SANDALIOS BROKHOS
(INCORRECT)

MS. GREC 2248 C. 1500

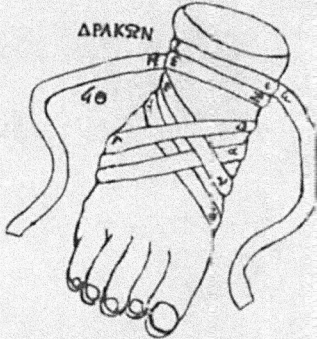

ΔΡΑΚΩΝ

V DRAKON BROKHOS (INCORRECT)

ΑΠΛΟΥΝ ΑΜΜΑ

Ρ ΑΝΙΣΟΤΟΝΟ

VI HAPLOUN HAMMA BROKHOS (INCORRECT)

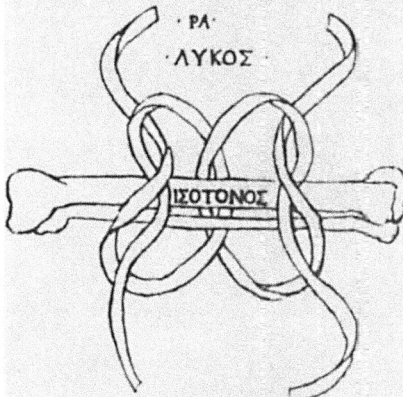

· ΡΑ· ·ΛΥΚΟΣ·

ΙΣΟΤΟΝΟΣ

VII LYKOS BROKHOS (INCORRECT)

ΗΡΑΚΛΕΩΤΙΚΟΝ ΑΜΜΑ

ΡΒ·

ΙΣΟΤΟΝΟΣ

VIII HERAKLEOTIKON HAMMA (INCORRECT)

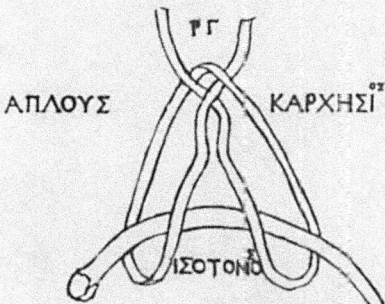

ΡΓ ΑΠΛΟΥΣ ΚΑΡΧΗΣΙ

ΙΣΟΤΟΝΟ

IX HAPLOUS KARKHESIOS (INCORRECT)

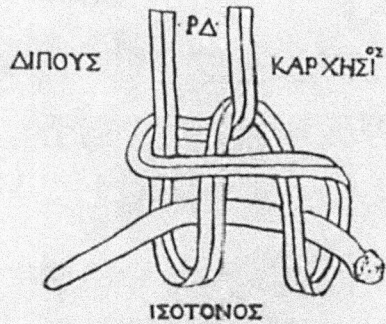

ΔΙΠΟΥΣ ΡΔ· ΚΑΡΧΗΣΙ

ΙΣΟΤΟΝΟΣ

X-XII DIPLOUS KARKHESIOS (INCORRECT)

133

MS. GREC 2248 C. 1500

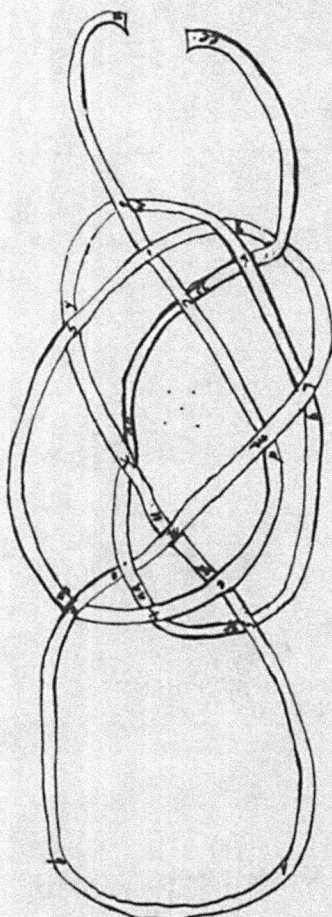

ΠΛΙΝΘΙΟΣ;ΤΕΤΡΑΚΥΚ ΟΚΑΙ

· P Z ·

ΙΣΟΤΟΝΟΣ

XIII   PLINTHIOS BROKHOS
(INCORRECT)

ΕΠΑΓΚΥΛΩΤΟΣ

X-XII   DIPLOUS KARKHESIOS
(INCORRECT)

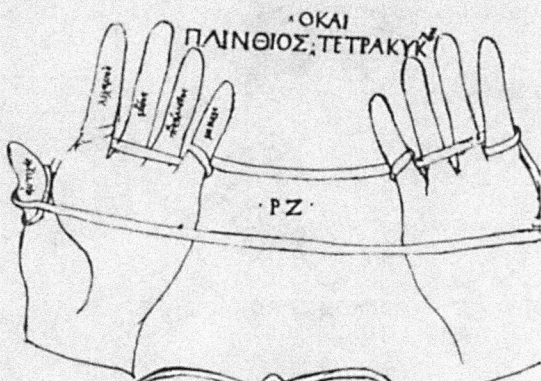

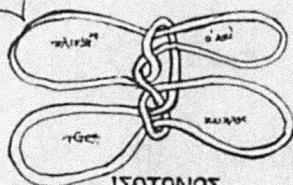

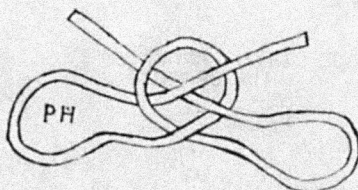

XIV   EPANKYLOTOS BROKHOS
(INCORRECT)

MS. GREC 2248 C. 1500

ΩΤΑ

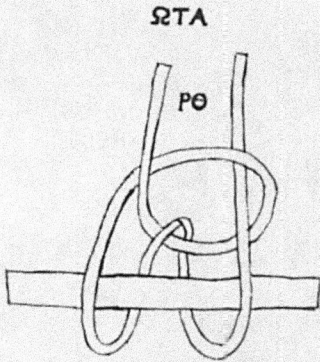

ΡΘ

XV OTA BROKHOS
(INCORRECT)

ΔΙΑΓΚΥΛΟΣ ΟΝΤΙΝΕΣ ΑΓΧΟΝ ΚΑΛΟΥΣΙΝ

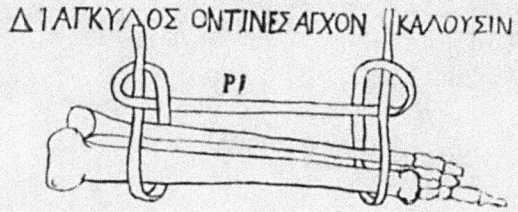

ΡΙ

XVI DIANKYLOS BROKHOS
(INCORRECT)

ΚΥΡΙΩΣ ΑΓΧΩΝ

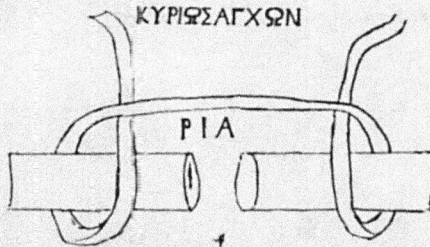

ΡΙΑ

XVII ANKHON BROKHOS
(INCORRECT)

ΥΠΕΡΒΑΤ

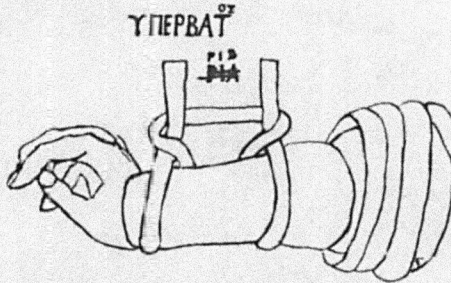

XVIII HYPERBATOS BROKHOS
(INCORRECT)

MS. LATIN 6866 C. 1540

Oribasius de laqueis ex Heracle Vidor Vidio Florétino interprete

Quæ ratio sit laquei Attollentis

I
ERTOS
BROKHOS
(CORRECT)

Quomodo laqueus Nauticus debeat adhiberi.

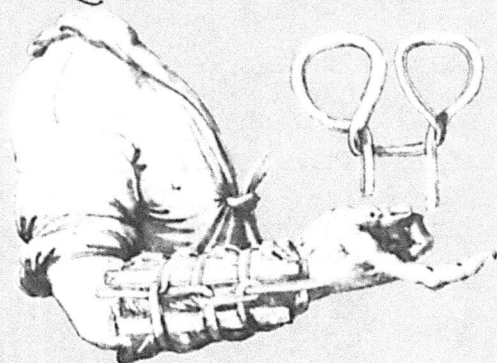

II
NAUTIKOS
BROKHOS
(INCORRECT)

Laqueus Xiasòs quomodo implicetur.

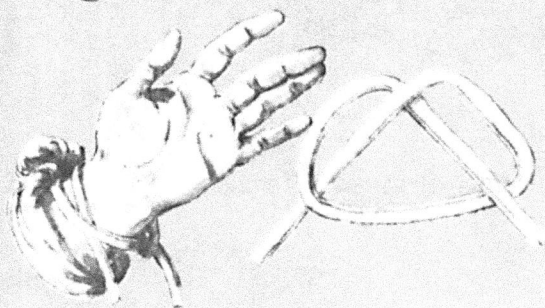

III
CHIESTOS
BROKHOS
(INCORRECT)

MS. LATIN 6866 C. 1540

Pastoralis laqueus, qui et sandalius dicitur quomo myciatur.

IV
SANDALIOS
BROKHOS
(INCORRECT)

Draco   *laqueus qua ua myciatur.*

V
DRAKON
BROKHOS
(INCORRECT)

Qua ratione u laqueus adhibeatur quem simplice nodu dixerut

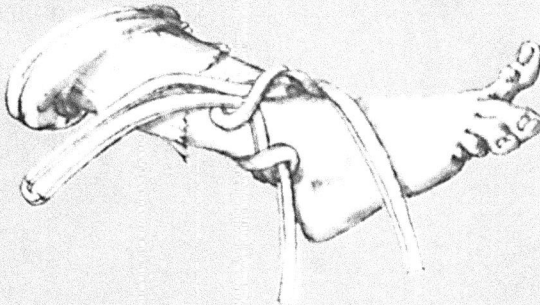

VI
HAPLOUN
HAMMA
BROKHOS
(INCORRECT)

MS. LATIN 6866 C. 1540

Lupus laqueus quomodo nectatur.

VII
LYKOS
BROKHOS
(INCORRECT)

Nodi Hercules ratio

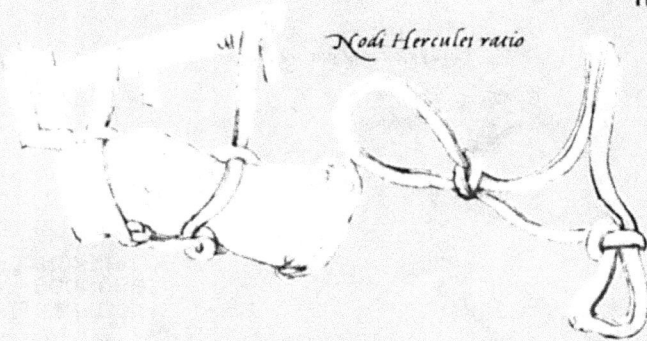

VIII
HERKLEOTIKON
HAMMA
(INCORRECT)

Simplex Charchesius qua via implicetur.

IX
HAPLOUS
KARKHESIOS
(INCORRECT)

MS. LATIN 6866 C. 1540

Duplex Charchesius, quo modo implicetur.

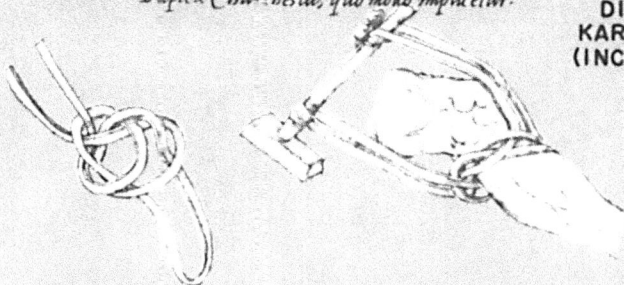

X
DIPLOUS
KARKHESIOS
(INCORRECT)

Duplex Charchesius quomó ex simplici fiat.

XI
DIPLOUS
KARKHESIOS
(INCORRECT)

Duplex Charchesius quomodo implicetur circúponédo.

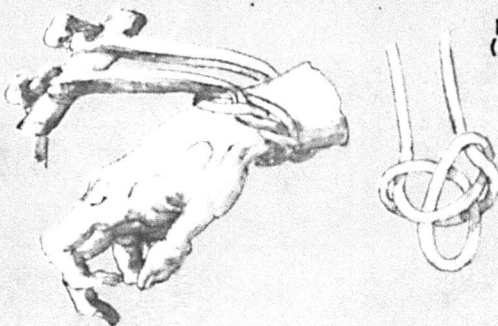

XII
DIPLOUS
KARKHESIOS
(INCORRECT)

MS. LATIN 6866 C. 1540

Laterculi qui alioquin quadruplex arculus dicit quae rosit

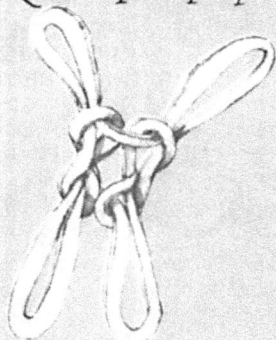

XIII
PLINTHIOS
BROKHOS
(INCORRECT)

Laqueus Epangylotus (ita
sup s mu injcitur) qua via

em appellat qm sins ?
mseri possit

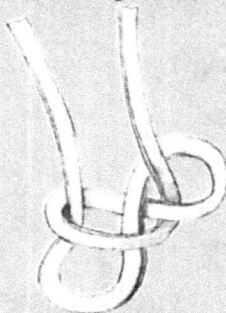

XIV
EPANKYLOTOS
BROKHOS
(INCORRECT)

Ratio eius laquei quem Auriculas micupat

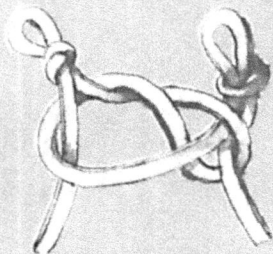

XV
OTA
BROKHOS
(INCORRECT)

MS. LATIN 6866 C. 1540

Laqueus duos habens smus quem nonnulli minus proprie
Strangulantem dixerut quomodo mijciatur

XVI
DIANKYLOS
BROKHOS
(INCORRECT)

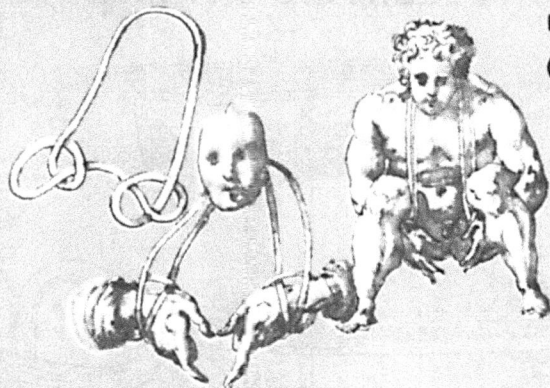

Ratio laquei quem Strangulantem proprie nuicupant

XVIII
HYPERBATOS
BROKHOS
(INCORRECT)

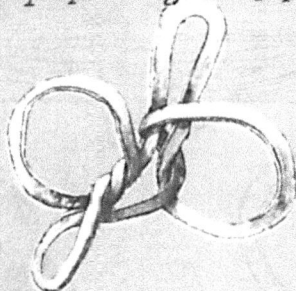

Quomodo adhibeatur laqueus ὑπέρβαλῖος, id em
nomen traxit ab eo q, supra feratur.

XVII
ANKHON
BROKHOS
(INCORRECT)

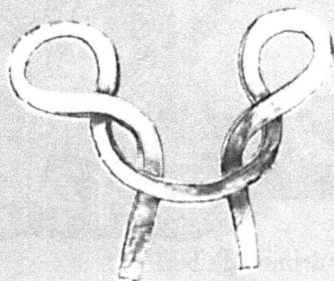

CHIRURGIA 1544

Oribaſius de laqueis ex Heracle Vi-
DO VIDIO FLORENTINO INTERPRETE.

Quæ ratio ſit laquei attollentis.

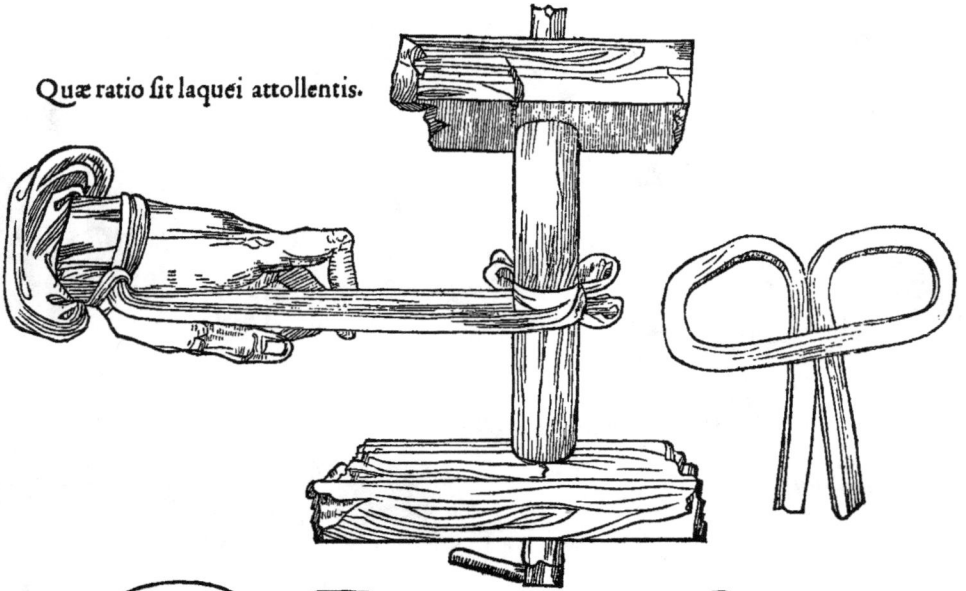

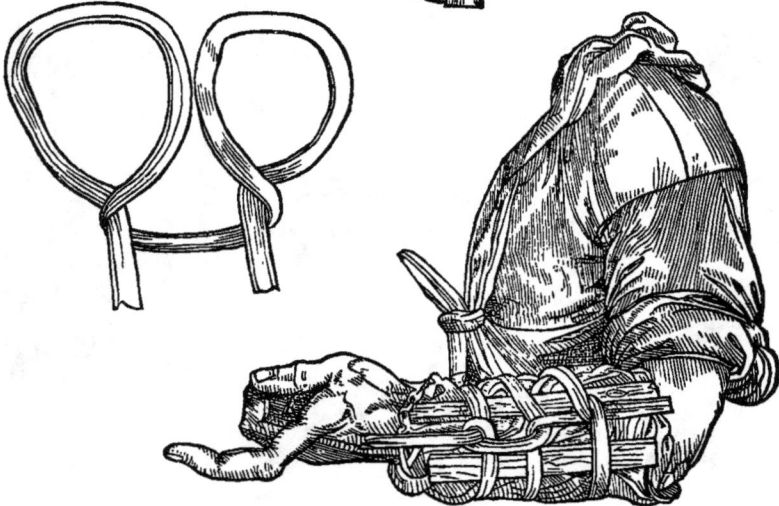

Quomodo laqueus Nauticus debeat adhiberi

CHIRURGIA 1544

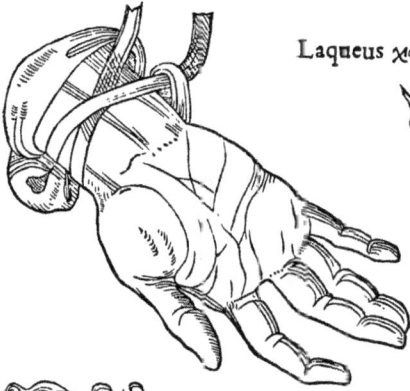

Laqueus χιασὸς quomodo implicetur.

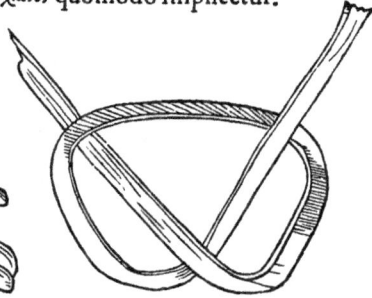

Paſtoralis laqueus,qui & Sandalius
dicitur,quomodo inijciatur.

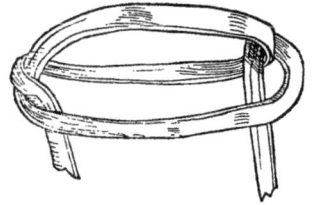

Draco laqueus,quâ viâ inijciatur.

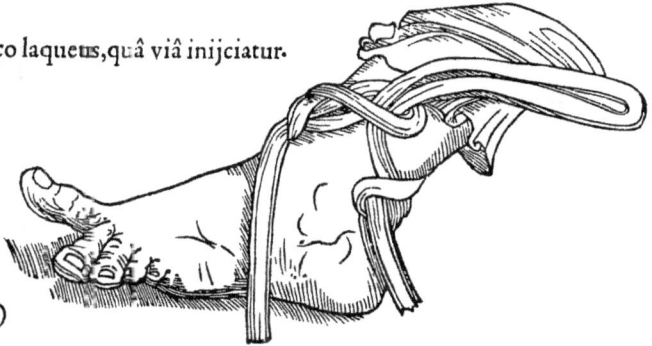

Qua ratione is laqueus adhibeatur,quem
ſimplicem nodum dixerunt.

CHIRURGIA 1544

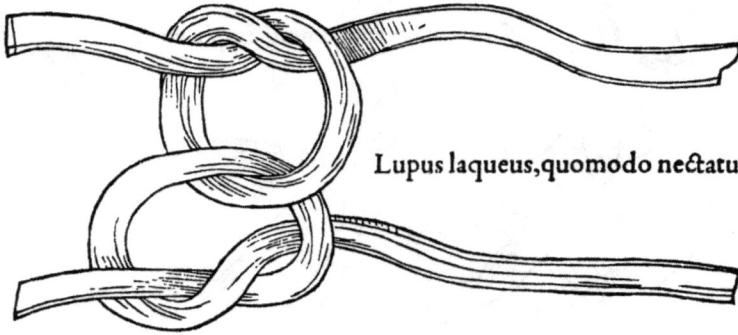

Lupus laqueus, quomodo nectatur.

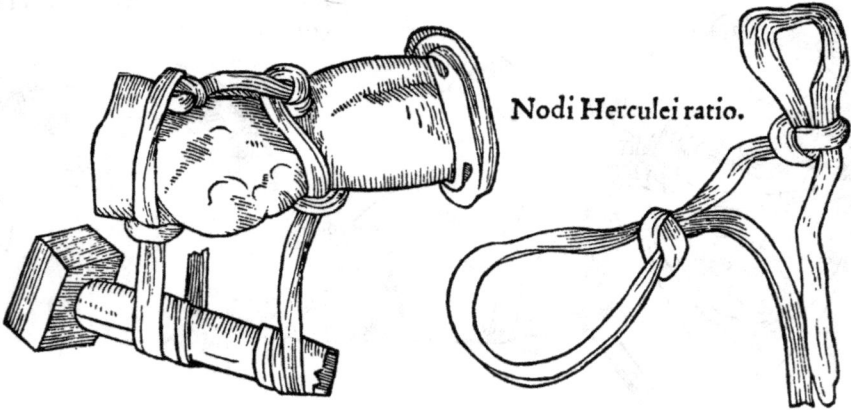

Nodi Herculei ratio.

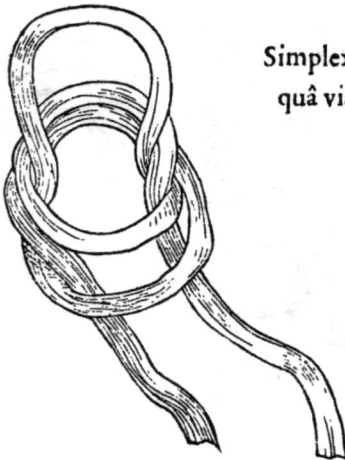

Simplex charchesius,
quâ viâ implicetur.

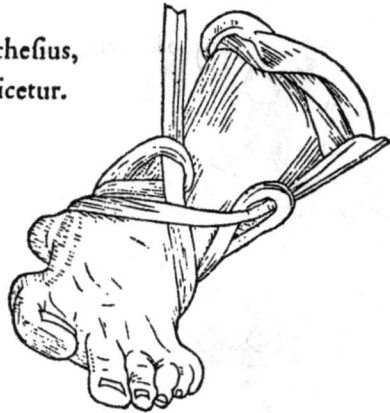

CHIRURGIA 1544

Duplex charchesius quo
modo implicetur.

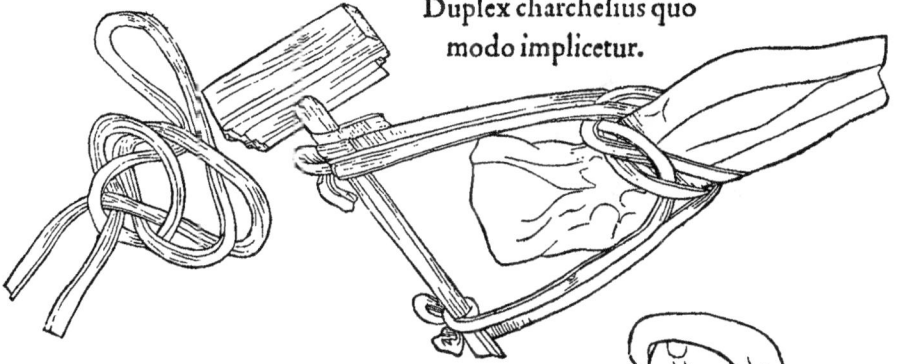

Duplex charchesius,quo
modo ex simplici fiat.

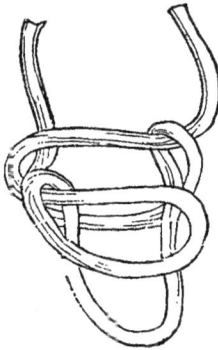

Duplex charchesius,
quomodo implicetur
circumponendo.

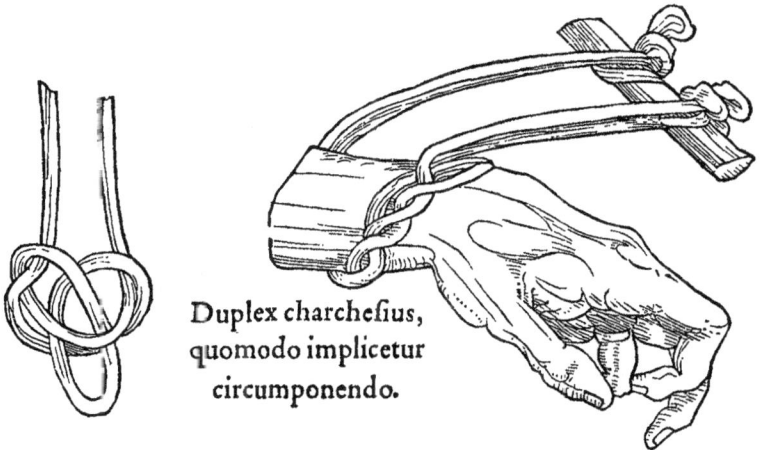

CHIRURGIA 1544

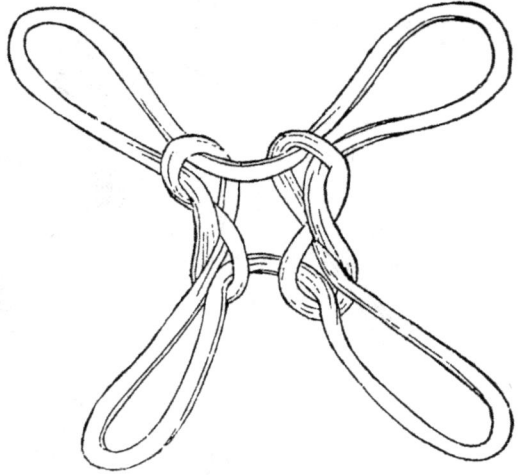

Plinthij,quod alioquin quadruplex
circulus dicitur, quæ ratio fit.

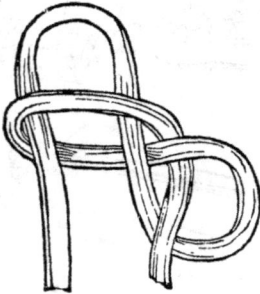

Laqueus Epangylotus (ità enim ap-
pellatur,quoniam finus fuper finum
inijcitur)quâ viâ inferi poffit.

CHIRURGIA 1544

Ratio eius laquei,quem auriculas nuncupant.

Laqueus duos habens ſinus(quem nonnulli minùs propriè ſtrangulantem dixerunt)quomodo inijciatur.

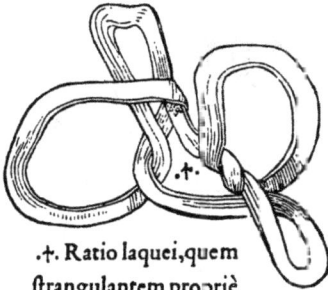

.✝. Ratio laquei,quem
ſtrangulantem propriè
nuncupant.

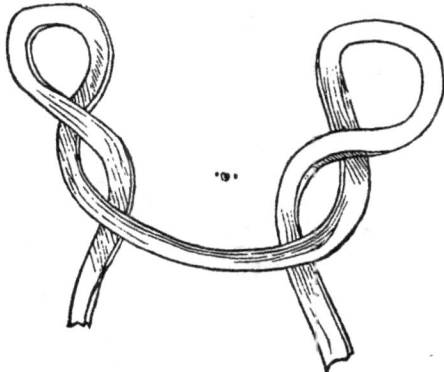

.ω.Quomodo adhibeatur laqueus ὑπέρβαϑς,id enim
nomen traxit ex eo,quòd ſupra feratur.

147

BUSSEMAKER & DAREMBERG 1861

BUSSEMAKER AND DAREMBERG'S IDENTÌFICATIONS
(DRAWINGS BY P. LACKERBAUER)

1. Lacs tressé (Chapter 1): From MS. Grec 2248. Correct.
2. Lacs des marins (Chapter 2): From MS. Grec 2248. Incorrect.
3. Lacs croisé (Chapter 3): From MS. Latin 6866. Incorrect.
4. Lacs du bouvier (Chapter 4): From MS. Latin 6866. Incorrect.
5. Dragon (Chapter 5): From MS. Latin 6866. Incorrect.
6. Noeud simple (Chapter 6): From MS. Grec 2248. Incorrect.
7. Loup (Chapter 7): From MS. Grec 2248. Incorrect.
8. Noeud d'Héraclée (Chapter 8): From MS. Grec 2248. Incorrect.
9. Câble simple (Chapter 9): From MS. Latin 6866. Incorrect.
10. Autre noeud d'Héraclée (Chapter 8): From MS. Latin 6866. Incorrect.
11. Câble double (Chapters 10-12): From MS. Latin 6866. Incorrect.
12. Autre câble simple (Chapter 9): From MS. Grec 2248. Incorrect.
13. Autre câble double (Chapters 10-12): From MS. Grec. 2248. Incorrect.
14. Plinthius à quatre cercles (Chapter 13): From MS. Latin 6866. Incorrect.
15. Autre espèce de plinthius (Chapter 13): From MS. Grec 2248. Incorrect.
16. Lacs à deux anses ou étrangleur (Chapter 16): From MS. Grec 2248. Incorrect.
17. Lacs à anses superposées (Chapter 14): From MS. Latin 6866. Incorrect.
18. Lacs transgressif (Chapter 18): From MS. Grec 2248. Incorrect.
19. Oreilles (Chapter 15): From MS. Latin 6866. Incorrect.
20. Étrangleur proprement dit (Chapter 17). From MS. Latin 6866. Incorrect.

ÖHRVALL 1916

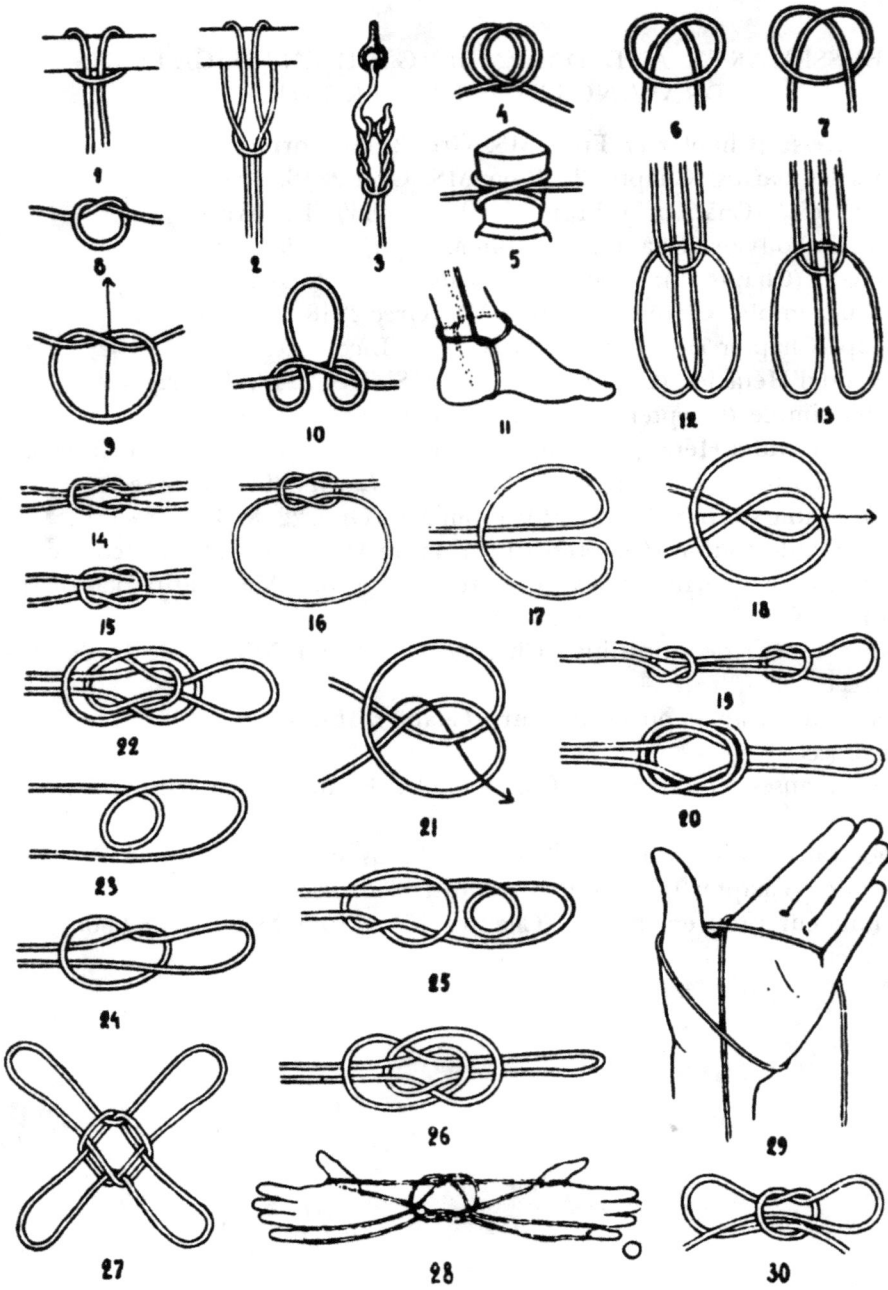

ÖHRVALL'S IDENTIFICATIONS (DRAWINGS BY E. ÖHRVALL)

1. Lärkhufvud.
2. Enkelt taljerepsstek (Chapter 1). Incorrect.
3. Dubbelt taljerepsstek.
4, 5. Sjömansknut (Chapter 2). Correct.
6, 7, 8. Öfverhandsknut (Chapter 3). Incorrect.
9, 10, 11. Påslagning (Chapter 4). Incorrect.
12, 13. (Chapter 5). Incorrect.
14. Lodstek (Chapter 7). Correct.
15. Käringknut.
16. Råbandsknut (Chapter 8). Correct.
17, 18, 19, 20. Kärleksknut (Chapter 9). Correct.
21-26. Säckknut (Chapter 10-12). Correct.
27. Trådfigur (Chapter 13). Correct.
28. Trådfigur från Queensland.
29, 30. Öfverhandsknut med öglor (Chapter 14). Correct.

Index

Abacus: etymology of, 12-13; Inca variety of, 31, 32, 35-38

Abba Thulle, Palau Island king: knot-calendar of, 5

Abramelin the Sage: on wizards' knots, 73

Acosta, Father José de: on the Inca abacus, 32-33, 36

Adair, James: on North American Indian knot-calendars, 3-4

Æolus: winds tied by, 44; mentioned, 45

Alcmena: bewitched by Ilithyia, 74

Al-Khwarizmi: on mathematical "units, knots, and composites," 13

Altieri, R. A.: on the colors of quipus, 18

Amulets: linguistic kinship of, to words denoting knots, 51-52; knots used as, 52, 53, 54, 68, 69, 70

Ankhon brokhos: Heraklas's description of, 129-130; diagram of, 130; identified, 130

Ankh sign: amuletic significance of, 52

Apellides, 112

Aphrodite: magic girdle of, 52

Arapaho Indians: knot-records of, 10

Archconfraternity of the Cord of Saint Joseph: knotted cord worn by members of, 78

Archimedes, 112

Asclepiadae: proprietary exclusiveness of, 89

Ashley, Clifford: on secret knots, 90; anthropological significance of book by, 91; on constrictor knot, 111

Assyria. *See* Babylonia and Assyria

Astronomy: Inca observations recorded on quipus, 19-31 *passim*; achievements of Mayan Indians and Stonehenge Britons, 20, 23, 26-30 *passim*. *See also* Eclipses, Planets

Athena: girdle of, tied by Hercules knot, 54, 55

Athenaeus: on Hercules vases, 62

Athenagoras: on Hercules knot, 62

Ayala, Huaman Poma de. *See* Huaman Poma de Ayala

Babylonia and Assyria: magic knots in, 46-50 *passim*, 67, 73

Bale, John: on Saint Wilfrid's knots, 78

Barrel knot (blood knot): secret of, 90

Barton's handerchief or cravat of the heel: *sandalios brokhos* similar to, 89, 114

Belt of Saint Guthlac: therapeutic power of, 78

Bennet, George. *See* Tyerman, Daniel, and Bennet, George

Bird, Junius, 22, 23

Birkelund, Palle, 31

Blackman, Winifred: on rosaries, 14

Blood knot. *See* Barrel knot (blood knot)

Boas, Franz: on Eskimo knots, 84; mentioned, 87

Bodin, Jean: on ligatures, 71

Bottle sling. *See* Jug sling

Boukolikos brokhos. See Sandalios brokhos *(boukolikos brokhos)*

Bowline knot: diagrams of, 83, 84; Eskimo variety of, 84, 85; mentioned by Captain John Smith, 100n*43*; mentioned, 82. *See also* Running bowline knot

Brahmans: ritual knots of, 76, 77

Buck, P. H., 84

Bulla: worn by Roman boys, 68

Burns, Robert: on ligatures, 41, 72

Bussemaker, U. C., and Daremberg, C. V.: edition of Oribasius by, 105, 106, 108, 117, 121, 131, 148

Calendar Round: borrowed from Mayas, 28; marked by knots in Mexico, 40

Carter, Howard: knot-amulets found by, 53

Cartouches: amuletic purpose of, 52

Cat's cradles. *See* String figures

Chasqui: functions of, 31, 32; Huaman Poma's drawing of, 35

Chaytor, A. H.: barrel knot published by, 90

Chiestos brokhos: Heraklas's description of, 112; diagrams of, 112; identified, 112-113; mentioned, 114, 117, 120, 128, 129

Fletcher, Giles, the elder: on wind-knots, 45

Francis I, king of France: translation of Oribasius sponsored by, 103; mentioned, 86

Frazer, Sir J. G.: on the principles of magic, 42; on Finnish wizards, 46; on therapeutic knots, 49; on magic knots, 70; on loosing knots at weddings, 73

Friis, Peder C.: on a Lapp's wind-knots, 45

Fringes. *See* Knotted fringes

Gandz, Solomon: on phylacteries and fringes, 11-12; on knotted strings as computers, 12-14; on relationship of knots and amulets, 51-52; on origin of phylacteries, 77

Garcilaso de la Vega, "el Inca": on the Inca decimal system, 15; on Inca astronomy, 19, 28; on eclipses, 30, 31; on Inca census, 38-39; on *quipucamayus*, 39-40

Gaston, Raphael: on constrictor knot, 111

Gay, John: on love knots, 75

Gerdy's extension knot: similarity of, to *drakhon brokhos*, 89, 115

Geryon: knots and arabesques on back of, 78

Goldsmith, Oliver: on love knots, 75

Gordian knot: secrecy of, 89; structure of, 98n*3*; mentioned, 88

Gorgon's head: amuletic power of, 62

Granny knot: presumed antiquity of, 81; contrasted with square knot, 82; diagram of, 83; allegedly tied by gorillas, 98n*6*

Graumont, Raoul, and Hensel, John: on secret knots, 89-90

"Gustavus Vasa," Swedish war ship: knots found on, 100n*43*

Hackamore. *See* Jug sling

Haddon, Kathleen: on string figures, 126

Hair: role of, in magic, 42, 49, 50

Half hitch: used by Hidatsa Indians, 82; diagram of, 83; distinguished from single hitch, 98n*4*

Handy, W. C., 84

Haploun hamma brokhos: Heraklas's description of, 115; diagram of, 115; identified, 116; mentioned, 113, 118

Havasupai Indians. *See* Pueblo Indians

Hawkins, Gerald: on the Stonehenge eclipse cycle, 29, 30

Heliodorus, Greek physician: treatise on machines by, 104, 109, 111, 120, 121, 129, 131

Hensel, John. *See* Graumont, Raoul, and Hensel, John

Heraklas, Greek physician: significance of, 86-91 *passim*, 103-106 *passim*; literal translation of treatise by, 107-131 *passim*

Herakleotikon hamma brokhos: Heraklas's description of, 117-118; diagram of, 117; identified, 118; contrasted with *lykos brokhos*, 118. *See also* Hercules knot and Square knot (reef knot)

Herakles. *See* Hercules

Hercules: supposed inventor of Hercules knot, 54; lion's skin of, tied with Hercules knot, 55, 61; birth of, impeded by magic, 74

Hercules knot: used as amulet in Egypt, 53, 57, 63; Pliny's praise of, 53; realistically portrayed in ancient art, 54-57; symbolism of, 62. *See also* Square knot (reef knot) and *Herakleotikon hamma brokhos*

Herodotus: on Darius's knot-calendar, 2; on Xerxes's bridge of boats, 85-86

Higden, Ranulf: on Manx wind-knots, 44

Himanteligmos: Greek knot game, 88

Hitches: presumed antiquity of, 81. *See also* Half hitch

Hogben, Lancelot: on magic numbers, 20

Homeopathic (imitative) magic: Frazer's definition of, 42

Homer, 46. *See also* Ulysses

Huaman Poma de Ayala: on Inca astronomy, 19; on eclipses, 30, 31; on the Inca abacus, 31, 37; drawings of Inca life by, 32-35; on the Inca decimal system, 37; mentioned, 39

Huayna Capac, Inca, 14, 15

Hubert, H.: on *mana* in magic, 42

Huichol Indians: knot-records used by, 4, 9

Hyperbatos brokhos: Heraklas's description of, 130; diagram of, 130; identified, 131

Illness. *See* Therapeutic knots

Imitative magic. *See* Homeopathic (imitative) magic

Isaiah: magic knots denounced by, 51

Isbuster, Helen: tried as witch, 7

Isis knot: statues of Isis identified by, 60, 65

Izze-kloth, Apache medicine cord: magic powers of, 49

James I, king of England: ligatures denounced by, 71

Jackson, Old Sally: knot-record made by, 4

Jackson, Robert: on the Inca abacus, 37

Jar sling. *See* Jug sling

www.ingramcontent.com/pod-product-compliance
Lightning Source LLC
Chambersburg PA
CBHW070344270326
41926CB00017B/3975